GRACEFUL REASON

GRACEFUL REASON

THE CONTRIBUTION OF REASON TO THEOLOGY

J. V. Langmead Casserley

FOREWORD BY JOHN HEUSS

GREENWICH · CONNECTICUT 1954

FOREWORD

The Rev. Dr. J. V. Langmead Casserley is rapidly becoming one of the most important teachers at work in the Protestant Episcopal Church. It was little more than a year ago that he came to the United States from England. I cannot recall anyone from our sister Communion, the Church of England, who has made such a distinguished and respected place for himself so quickly in our midst. He was known, when his election as the Mary Crooke Hoffman Professor of Dogmatic Theology at the General Theological Seminary was announced in 1952, to a small group of Episcopalians who had read and appreciated his earlier books. Today, his reputation as a brilliant, witty, and profound theological thinker and lecturer is strongly established.

It is always a tribute of more than considerable proportions when a profound theologian begins to be in wide demand as a speaker to clerical and lay groups. The popular mind, unfortunately, has been conditioned to expect theology to be dull and irrelevant, because more often than we like to think, it has been the personality of the theologian that has been dull. The quick response which the Church public in this section of America has given to Dr. Casserley is, on the one hand, convincing evidence that people want to get theological meat to chew on, and on the other hand, that when the right man comes along they will listen with intelligent understanding and appreciation. All of us who have watched this small miracle take place have fairly burst with decorous Episcopal delight that Dr. Casserley belongs to the Anglican Communion and at least for a few years, we trust, to the American Episcopal Church.

In addition to seminary teaching, extensive preaching, and lecturing at conferences of various sorts, Dr. Casserley now brings out an excellent book. This is no mean accomplishment, because when one has become endeared to the American Church public as quickly and as solidly as Dr. Casserley has, there is precious little time left to do much writing.

The book is about the delicate and touchy problem of the place and importance of Natural Theology. It is significant because the question of the proper relationship between theology and philosophy comes very close to being the formidable fence over which honest advocates of differing theological viewpoints eye one another with the greatest suspicion today. Dr. Tillich understood this very well when he wrote the first volume of his *Systematic Theology*. Dr. Casserley is grateful to Dr. Tillich for pointing his finger at the area of greatest theological sensitivity, but he does not believe that the cure which is suggested will bring the needed healing. He believes that there is place for a roomier mutual collaboration between the philosopher and the theologian than Dr. Tillich's suggested method affords. This book will deserve and get much study and discussion on this point alone from the technical experts in both fields of thought.

Yet, it would be a great shame if *Graceful Reason* were read only by the highbrow set, even if the ideas which they wrestle with on their particular Mount Olympus do in time trickle down to shape the pedestrian minds of all of the rest of us. Without losing one ounce of intellectual force, Dr. Casserley has a way of writing which any reasonably educated man can quickly grasp. As one who has to interpret theology daily to the man in the street, I find all that he writes useful grist for my humble mill.

The street where my mill does its grinding happens to be Wall Street, where the shepherd cares little if his sheep are often mistakenly called wolves by some, and bulls or bears by others. One mental characteristic, however, predominates on this street. People here are realists and they are in a hurry. When they ask questions, they expect relevant and practical answers. I am grateful to the author of this book, not only for coming down to Old Trinity frequently to speak directly to our congregations, but also for supplying me through his clear writing with some more food for my zoo-like part of the vineyard. I believe that when you read what he has set down here, you will be grateful, too.

JOHN HEUSS

Epiphany, 1954

CONTENTS

CONTENTS

xii

INTRODUCTION

Every system of theology, or essay in theological thinking, is compelled in some way or other to relate itself and its findings or contentions to philosophy. Although theology is very different from philosophy there is a considerable overlap or convergence of interest which links them together. Many, although by no means all, of the questions discussed by philosophers, and particularly by the very great philosophers—questions about the meaning and purpose of human existence, about ultimate reality and absolute truth, and whether and how man can know them—are also questions necessarily discussed, from their own point of view, by theologians. Thus, the theologian can never entirely ignore philosophy. He can take up a negative or sceptical attitude toward it, but a negative or sceptical attitude toward philosophy is itself a form of philosophy, although in the opinion of most of the very greatest philosophers not a very competent or satisfying form.

In most of the classical systems of theology the department of the subject which overlaps with philosophy, and in which the theologian makes his own philosophical position clear, is usually called natural theology. The traditional view, found in the writings of almost all Catholic theologians and not a few Protestants, is that philosophy at its best, the greatest philosophers in their highest moments, is characterized by a recognizable movement in what we may call a Godward direction. Some hold that philosophy can even conclusively demonstrate the existence of God, while others content themselves with the more moderate view that philosophy can at least indicate that the existence of God is a much more probable conclusion than any known alternative. Those theologians who are impressed by this widespread Godward movement in philosophy usually hold that it constitutes an important form of evidence which the Christian ought not to ignore. They argue that the Christian revelation indeed fulfils and goes far beyond the highest expectations of philosophy, but add that it does not overthrow them altogether.

Since the time of Emmanuel Kant, the great German critical philosopher, however, many Protestant theologians have taken the view that the final product of philosophical thought is a scepticism about the capacity of human reason to reach any kind of ultimate truth about the universe and the meaning of existence, and have concluded that the Christian theologian cannot rely upon or make any use of philosophy at all. Such theologians usually claim that they reject all forms of natural theology. Nevertheless, even they are compelled to relate their theological thinking to philosophy and to provide it with some kind of philosophical foundation—in this case, of course, a sceptical one.

It is no exaggeration to say that the fundamental distinction between theologians and schools of theological thinking today is that between those who believe that some kind of metaphysics is possible and valid within its limits and those who deny the possibility of any kind of metaphysics at all. The question of the validity of metaphysical philosophy is not, however, for most theologians a purely philosophical one. Each of these two contrasted positions has its own theological interpretation. Those who deny the competence and value of philosophy usually hold an extreme view of the Fall of man according to which that primordial tragedy had the effect, among its many other tragic consequences, of completely cutting off the human intellect from all ultimate reality and truth. Those, on the other hand, who tend to believe that some kind of metaphysical thinking is valid and possible take a slightly more moderate view of the Fall. They argue that it cruelly injured and viciously distorted all human activities, including rational thought, but they hold that the image of God in man still persists, so that here and there in human existence we can still observe and experience its reality. It is not easy, they say, for fallen man to use his intellect with complete honesty and integrity of method and purpose, but it is not altogether impossible, and sometimes it actually happens. Nevertheless, both those theologians who believe in some kind of natural theology and those who reject all kinds of natural theology have at least this in common: they both see the need for providing their theological thinking with some kind of philosophical foundation. Such a foundation is provided as much by a philosophical scepticism as by a formulated natural theology, and there can be no doubt that from the point of view of rounding off and completing a theological system, both philosophical scepticism on the one hand and the traditional natural theology on the other are about equally efficient.

Dr. Paul Tillich in the first volume of his *Systematic Theology* has proposed what is in effect a new way of trying to relate theology and philosophy via natural theology. For him it is the task of natural theology to ask the questions and the task of revealed theology to provide the answers. This way of relating the verdicts and illuminations of revealed or "supranatural" theology, as he terms it, to the rational questions which result from our attempt to analyze our own experience, he calls "the method of correlation."

The method of correlation is an interesting and often important conception which will, I believe, contribute in many ways to the development of the logical structure of theological thought and discussion in the future. But I do not believe it is strong enough to bear the whole burden of the relationship between theology and philosophy. Natural theology cannot be defined, as Dr. Tillich seems to imply, simply in terms of a method of correlation. "The method of correlation," he says, "solves this historical and systematic riddle [that is, the problem of natural theology and its relation to Christian revelation] by resolving natural theology into the analysis of existence and by resolving supranatural theology into the answers given to the questions implied in existence." [1]

The limitations of the method are brought out clearly enough when we see that the analysis of existence produces not only questions which call for a theological answer but also insights and verdicts which require a theological interpretation, a very different thing. Conversely, revealed or supranatural theology itself, not only supplies us with answers to our existential questions, but also raises questions which call for a philosophical and often an existential answer.

The true relationship between philosophy and theology is one of more equal collaboration in which questions are raised by both sides and answers are required of both sides. It would seem to me, therefore, that Dr. Tillich's interesting and important method of correlation does not really solve the problem of whether in the long run we should relate philosophy and theology on the basis of a sceptical and critical philosophy which dares affirm no metaphysical proposition or whether we should relate them on the basis of a philosophy which, however cautiously, still ventures to believe in the possibility of valid metaphysical insights and discoveries.

But a natural theology has one advantage that philosophical scepticism does not possess. It provides the Christian thinker with a point of contact or convergence with non-Christian thought which, from the apologetic point of view, may be of the greatest philosophical importance.

[1] Paul Tillich, *Systematic Theology* (Chicago: University of Chicago, 1951), I, 65-66.

It seems to me that the greatest danger at the present time is the development of a situation in which the Christian thinker and the non-Christian thinker have nothing whatever to say to each other because there is nothing about which they are agreed and no theme in which they share a common interest.

Those of us who are interested in the possibility of keeping alive an intelligible discussion between the Church and the world—and surely all Christians must be vitally interested in such a possibility—cannot ignore or take a negative attitude toward the questions raised by natural theology.

In this book I have attempted to discuss the problem of natural theology almost entirely from this second point of view. I have said very little about the role and logical place of natural theology in systematic Christian theology. Instead, I have concentrated on describing some of the varieties of natural theology and on evaluating them primarily from the point of view of their usefulness in the field of Christian propaganda and rational apologetics. But the question of natural theology is not only of an intellectual or even practical importance; it is also one with which we find certain very real ecumenical overtones connected.

The Anglican, as he looks out upon the surrounding theological world, sees that the whole problem of the nature and status of natural theology is one of those issues about which Christians are divided. This division, however fundamental in itself, is symptomatic of much more profound divisions. As I understand it, it belongs to the very office of an Anglican (it is part of the inherent function of an Anglican within Christendom) to address himself particularly, in an irenical and peacemaking mood, to any of those great controversies in which he sees Christians who stand, so to speak, to the right or the left of him hotly engaged. Always to stand in the middle of violent contestants and speak a word of peace is of course a dangerous vocation, but it seems inherent in what we may call the Anglican situation —or better, perhaps, the Anglican predicament! In any case, it is in this mood that I approach the present problem.

When I discuss theological issues with leading and gifted Roman Catholic theologians, I am impressed with the strength of the case for some sort of natural theology. Turning, on the other hand, to theologians of the Reformed persuasions, I am similarly impressed by many of the criticisms which they make of natural theology in what I may venture to call "its received Roman Catholic form."

As an Anglican, I feel that it is my duty to attempt some kind of restatement in an endeavor to meet some of the criticisms (though we shall probably have to confess that it is not possible, and perhaps not even necessary, to meet them all) and to bridge the gap. As I say, it is inherent in the Anglican situation that we should spend the whole of our existence toilsomely building bridges, and then standing in the middle of them, facing in both directions. The reader will agree that from the physiological point of view this is an extremely exacting operation! Nevertheless, it is to such an office that the Holy Spirit of God has called us in the Anglican communion, and by our Anglican allegiance we are committed to it. This is indeed no small vocation, and certainly not one for which we need apologize to any man.

This book is based on the Reinecker Lectures given early

in 1953 to students of the Episcopal Theological Seminary at Alexandria, Virginia. I have expanded the lectures somewhat in order to give them a more literary form, and I have added a fair amount of new material, but I hope that something of their original purpose and intention has survived the process. The lectures were given to students and not to or for expert philosophers and theologians. No doubt some of the students were, and some of them may become, expert philosophers or theologians, but I have had to deal with students so long that they no longer trail any clouds of intellectual glory for me. Most of them are ordinary people who happen to be studying, so that there need be very little difference between a lecture or a book intended for a student audience and a lecture or a book intended for any audience of generally well-educated people motivated by a genuine interest in the kind of question which the lecture or book discusses.

In other words, because the lectures were originally given to students, this book which has grown out of them is essentially a book for the general reader, and it is as such that I venture to hope that it will be received by such a public as it attracts and enjoys.

CHAPTER ONE

A DESCRIPTION OF NATURAL THEOLOGY

What is Natural Theology?

There can be no simple answer. Natural theology is not a specific and unchanging form of doctrine which can be written down, discussed, and criticized once and for all. On the contrary, it is a particular kind of Christian intellectual activity which has assumed many different forms in the past and may, for all we know, assume new forms in the future of which at present we can have no conception. As new points of view arise and establish themselves in philosophy and the sciences, they present new opportunities to the natural theologian, so that not only is his task never finished, but it has always to be started all over again.

Nevertheless, I think it possible to discern and describe at least four different ways of approaching and understanding natural theology, none of them adequate by itself, because usually any particular essay in natural theology is compounded and blended of various elements drawn from each type of approach. But it will be useful to describe briefly these four different ways of understanding natural theology as a prelude to the discussion of the whole subject which follows.

First, by natural theology we may mean any intellectual movement of the mind which is conceived to lie in a Godward direction, proceeding from some point or from many points in the immediate life and experience of man. It is thought that man undertakes such a movement of his mind because it is natural to man, because he is a specific kind of being—a being with an intellectual destiny orientated Godward, roughhew it how he may. From this point of view, some sort of Godward movement of the mind is natural to man because man, even fallen man, is a man made for God. It may be held that in proportion as his thinking has integrity and a genuine humanity, it will inevitably tend to take this generally Godward direction. Natural theology may be the development and verification of such an assumption as this.

Second, by natural theology we may mean some sort of argument, based on naturalistic premises, for the validity of religious behavior in general, for the existence of God or for the existence of a spiritual realm. I suppose the best-known arguments for the existence of God are of the cosmological kind—that immense variety or family of arguments which are basically of the form "because the world exists, God exists." No doubt this is the best-known kind of natural theology, so much so that many people think it is the only possible kind, but it is important for us to recognize at the

2

outset that there are in fact many kinds of natural theology of which this is only one, although certainly the most familiar.

Third, we may mean something quite different from either of the above. Natural theology may mean to us a theology of nature. This will not be an argument from nature to God, but an attempt to show that the theological categories of thought are adequate to the interpretation of nature and the natural sciences. This is a much less familiar conception, but I am quite certain that it is a theme which cannot be omitted in any attempt, however brief, to survey the scope and variety of natural theology.

The fourth approach is one peculiarly dear to the Anglican mind and the Anglican heart. It is the specifically Anglican form, a form classically expounded by one of the very greatest of the theologians of the Anglican tradition, Bishop Butler (though not by him alone). Here, natural theology takes the form of the tracing of an analogy between what I will call natural and evangelical experience. In Bishop Butler's *Analogy of Religion,* of course, we find this argument immediately related to eighteenth century controversies which are dead and gone. But that does not mean that the essential insights of the book are outmoded, though it may and does mean that it is now necessary for us to rethink and restate the argument in relation to twentieth century controversies of which Bishop Butler was necessarily ignorant.

As I have said, we should not suppose that this argument is peculiar to Bishop Butler alone. We find, for example, an excellent statement of the germ of it in a book published

two years before his. It will interest American readers to
know that it was written while the author was residing for
a short time in the United States. The book was the *Alciphron*
by Bishop George Berkeley, possibly the greatest contribution to Anglican divinity ever written in this country.
Berkeley writes: "It will be sufficient, if such analogy appears between the dispensations of grace and nature, as may
make it probable (although much should be unaccountable
in both) to suppose them derived from the same Author,
and the workmanship of one and the same Hand." [1]

This doctrine of the analogy between the realm of grace
and the realm of nature (between religious and physical
experience) must be very carefully distinguished from the
doctrine of analogical predication which we find in Thomas
Aquinas and other medieval writers. The doctrine of analogical predication asks and attempts to answer the question
how it is that we are able to use affirmative human language about God and yet avoid the danger of crude, or
even refined, anthropomorphism. The answer is given in
terms of a theory which traces and affirms analogies between
God and His creatures, while at the same time steadfastly
rejecting any kind of identity.

Although these are different theories, we would be mistaken in supposing that there is no connection at all between the two. In fact, we find in Berkeley's *Alciphron*, also,
a passage in which the author gives as lucid a summary
statement of the scholastic doctrine of analogical predication as can be found in the English language. Because of

[1] Arthur A. Luce and Thomas E. Jessop, ed., *Works of George Berkeley*
(Edinburgh: Nelson), III, 281. Used by permission of the publisher.

the intrinsic worth of this passage and because of the interesting way in which it betrays the familiarity of an eighteenth century Anglican bishop with medieval philosophy, I venture to quote a part of it.

Thomas Aquinas expresseth his sense of this point in the following manner. All perfections, saith he, derived from God to the creatures are in a certain higher sense, or (as schoolmen term it) eminently in God. Whenever, therefore, a name borrowed from any perfection in the creature is attributed to God, we must exclude from its signification every thing that belongs to the imperfect manner, wherein that attribute is found in the creature. Whence he concludes that knowledge in God is not a habit, but a pure act. And again, the same Doctor observes that our intellect gets its notions of all sorts of perfections from the creatures and that as it apprehends those perfections, so it signifies them by names. Therefore, saith he, in attributing these names to God, we are to consider two things; first, the perfections themselves, as goodness, life and the like, which are properly in God; and secondly, the manner which is peculiar to the creature, and cannot, strictly and properly speaking, be said to agree to the Creator. And although Suarez, with other schoolmen, teacheth, that the mind of man conceiveth knowledge and will to be in God as faculties or operations, by analogy only to created beings; yet he gives it plainly as his opinion, that when knowledge is said not to be in God, it must be understood in a sense including imperfection, such as discursive knowledge, or the like imperfect kind found in the creatures: and that, none of those imperfections in the knowledge of men or angels belonging to the formal notion of knowledge, or to knowledge as such, it will not thence follow that knowledge, in its proper formal sense, may not be attributed to God: and of knowledge taken in general for the clear evident understanding of all truth, he expressly affirms that it is in God, and that this was never denied by any philosopher who believed in God. It was, indeed, a current opinion in the schools, that even

5

being itself should be attributed analogically to God and the creatures. That is, they held that God, the supreme, independent, self-originate cause and source of all beings, must not be supposed to exist in the same sense with created beings, not that he exists less truly, properly, or formally, than they, but only because he exists in a more eminent and perfect manner.[2]

Thus, the doctrine of analogical predication, the doctrine that analogy is the proper means of religious communication, depends upon and presupposes a doctrine of analogy between natural and what I have called evangelical experience in the realities themselves.

It is possible for us to use analogy in our communications with one another only if reality itself is characterized by certain broad and profound analogical trends. In other words, we can draw analogies validly only if there are some real analogies to be drawn. So this particular form of the doctrine—an advance, as it seems to me, upon anything we find in Thomas himself except in the form of a mere hint—may validly be regarded as the specifically Anglican contribution to natural theology, the one which is peculiarly rooted in our own great intellectual traditions.

A Basis for Apologetics

Accompanying all forms of natural theology is the suggestion that a natural theology is normally and properly something conceived and elaborated by a Christian in faith. A natural theology is not first and primarily a ladder on which one climbs to faith but, on the contrary, something which the Christian, thinking in the tradition of faith, labors to construct for two reasons.

[2] *Ibid.,* 168 ff.

The first of these reasons is intellectual in character. He devises a natural theology in order to fill an indispensable niche in any adequate theological system. The second is of a practical, pastoral, and evangelical character. He elaborates a natural theology in order to establish a basis for carrying on conversation with a non-Christian or a sub-Christian man.

Although a natural theology is normally formulated by a Christian in faith, standing upon the faith, nevertheless, in its essential nature it is animated and motivated by a desire for conversation with those who lie outside the faith. Thus, it seizes gladly and avidly upon any point of convergence which it can find as it looks at the life and the thought of those who stand outside the Church (in the widest sense of the word).

But natural theology has also a positive function in relation to the life and thought of the faithful Christian himself. The Christian is never only or merely a Christian. He is also man: a vegetative animal living with nature; a social animal clashing and collaborating with his fellowman; an aesthetic creature, prizing and delighting in a conscious response to such of the beauties of life as he is capable of appreciating; a worker participating in some of the activities which constitute the life of his society. If he is a truly faithful Christian, no doubt his interests in Christianity will be the primary interest of his life; but even if he is a theologian, it will almost certainly not be his only interest. Indeed, in a theologian such a narrow concentration of interest would be deplorable.

Every Christian, in other words, shares some interests

with non-Christians. For his own sake, therefore, as well as theirs, he must find some positive and constructive way of relating such interests to his Christian faith. If he cannot relate his interests—philosophical, scientific, artistic, literary, political, or social—to his Christianity he will never succeed in becoming a complete and integrated Christian. He will live a mixed life, part Christian, part secular, spiritually torn asunder by motives and forms of conduct which he does not know how to harmonize with each other.

Precisely because the Christian man is also the natural man, he requires the guidance of a natural theology in order to remain at the same time one man, one Christian man completely devoted to the service of God within the context of his natural life, one natural man giving himself up entirely to the fulfilment of the purpose of the Creator of his nature. To use a piece of modern philosophical jargon, because the Christian man is also the natural man a natural theology is for him an existential necessity.

A Question of Fact

We may ask ourselves, do such points of convergence as those to which we have alluded exist? Indeed, there are some theologians who deny that they *can* exist. But, it seems to me, the question whether such points of convergence exist is primarily the empirical question: do we in fact encounter such points of convergence? and not the purely *a priori* question, *can* there be such points of convergence?

Some Biblical theologians try to show that there cannot be a natural theology simply by quoting appropriate pas-

8

sages of Scripture—and also, like so many Biblical theologians, by not quoting inappropriate passages of Scripture! But the question whether a natural theology exists is primarily a question of fact; do we discover points of convergence, not by reading the Bible, but by reading all sorts of other books? And surely the answer to that, by any honest mind that does read other books, can only be that in some sense we do.

Just as the Christian looking round about him in the world in which he lives, or studying history or the biographies of great men, often discovers in the lives of non-Christian men and women instances of conduct and high character which he cannot fail but admire, and cannot but admire precisely because he is a Christian, so will he often find in the writings of non-Christian thinkers affirmations and points of view with which, precisely because he is a Christian, he cannot but agree. Sometimes such writers will even say things which will lead him to a more profound understanding of the meaning of his own faith than he had before. Christian thought has never throughout its history been an isolated or introverted form of intellectualism, ignoring all but specifically Christian writings and specifically Christian thinkers.

The earliest Christian writers during the second century were influenced by the stoics and middle-platonists: Augustine by the neo-platonists; Thomas Aquinas by an epoch-making rediscovery of the text of Aristotle; and contemporary Christian philosophers by Darwin, the twentieth century physicists, and anti-Christian writers like Marx and Freud.

It seems to me undeniable that the living points of convergence, upon which natural theology seizes, exist today just as they have existed in the past. As long as such points of convergence exist, natural theology remains both a possible and a necessary activity.

A Warning and a Qualification

If the existence of these points of convergence is so obvious and undeniable, why is it that a considerable number of theologians refuse to allow that natural theology has any kind of validity at all? Partly no doubt, it is due to the belief of so many contemporary Protestant theologians that Christian theology ought to be not merely primarily Biblical in its inspiration and appeal but also exclusively Biblical in its foundation and method. For myself, I can find no ground either in the Bible itself or in the history of Christian thought or in what we may call Christian common sense for so rigidly exclusive a Biblicism as this. The issue first clearly arose and was formulated at the Council of Nicaea, when any narrow and exclusive Biblicism was decisively, and to my mind rightly, set aside.

However, this is not the kind of objection to natural theology which seems to me sufficiently important for discussion here. A better reason for distrusting natural theology is the suspicion that if there is a natural theology there must also be a natural religion which corresponds to it. This illusion, that the validity of natural theology implies the possibility of a merely natural religion, is the great mistake, in particular, of some of the natural theologians of the eighteenth century, and it seems to me that a distrust of natural theology is quite legitimate unless and until this particular illusion is clearly seen for what it is and set aside.

Natural theology, as I understand it, is necessarily a department of Christian theology, a phase of Christian intellectualism. It cannot compose or correspond to a religion because after all it consists of no more than a series of inferences, whereas a real living religion is not a series of inferences but a confrontation with reality. A living religion is something which happens, not when and because man infers (however valid his inferences may be), but when and because God acts and speaks. The great makers and architects of systems of natural theology, Thomas Aquinas, for example, see this clearly enough. For them the culminating point of natural theology is when it demonstrates the need for revelation. It shows the emptiness of a niche which philosophy can perceive but which it cannot fill. From this point of view natural theology has a relationship to the Christian revelation akin to that of the relationship of Hebrew prophecy to the great self-revealing acts of God in the life, death, and Resurrection of Jesus Christ.

Natural theology may indicate the need for revelation, and it may bring the philosophical man to a point where he is ready to listen to revelation, but it cannot act as a substitute for revelation. The relationship between the inferences of natural theology and the Christian revelation which confirms them, we will consider later on. It will be enough at this stage for us to see clearly that the possibility of a natural theology in no way implies the possibility of a natural religion. This being so, the one really important reason for the prevalent distrust of natural theology among contemporary theologians can safely be set aside.

Two Definitions

This section contains two brief essays in definition. We shall be concerned with the definition of two terms: "general revelation" and "nature."

The use of the terms general revelation and natural theology. A considerable number of recent theologians, while either denying or ignoring traditional natural theology, make a great play with what they call "general revelation." What is the relationship between general revelation and natural theology? Is it just another name for the same thing; is it a new name for some novel reinterpretation of the same thing; or is it an entirely independent concept?

The basic idea seems to be that nature does not so much prove or imply the existence of God (so that we can argue from nature to God) as declare or attest or make manifest the existence of God, so that we must say that in some sense all nature and experience speak to us of God.

"The heavens declare the glory of God, and the firmament showeth His handiwork," said the psalmist. One of the greatest scholastic philosophers and theologians, Bonaventura, laid great stress on the way in which nature directly manifests the glory of God, and many passages in Calvin reflect the same idea. Among Anglican theologians, Bishop Berkeley's conception of a natural, visual language, through which God speaks to us as step by step we experience the world around us, really amounts to very much the same thing as the modern conception of general revelation and even provides it with a philosophical basis which the doctrine sometimes lacks in the writings of contemporary theologians.

Quite clearly, all theologians, even those who believe in natural theology, will agree that the heavens do indeed declare the glory of God. There is no necessary contradiction or distinction between saying that nature proves or implies the divine existence and saying that nature manifests the divine glory. Indeed, it is easy to see that these two statements simply look at and report the same phenomenon from opposite sides. Nature can only make manifest the divine glory if it also proves or attests the divine existence. Conversely, if it proves or attests the divine existence, it also proclaims the divine glory. When we say that nature proclaims the divine glory, this can only be so because God is ultimately responsible for the existence of nature and because all reality which is other than God is God's handiwork. But if all existence which is not God is creaturely existence, then clearly all existence which is not God rationally implies the supreme reality of its Creator.

Natural theology looks at and formulates this fact in a philosophical way; general revelation contemplates and delights in it in a devotional way. Neither natural theology nor general revelation are possible apart from the other. No doubt, from the point of view of our spiritual and devotional life, general revelation is the more important of the two; but from the intellectual point of view, natural theology is prior to general revelation.

The heavens can only declare the glory of God if we already know that God exists. Once we know that God exists and is responsible for the existence of nature, then we see clearly enough that nature makes manifest His glory. The great natural theologians like Thomas Aquinas do indeed, without using the term, expound a doctrine of general revelation. For them, the fact that the creation makes manifest the glory of the Creator is the foundation of their whole doctrine of the analogy of being, which makes it possible for us to discover, within our experience of the creation, analogies or clues to the mystery of the being of God.

Thus, the concept of general revelation is quite useless to those theologians who wish to ignore or deny natural theology. Far from being an alternative that enables us to dispense with natural theology, it directly implies it. Indeed, it implies also that doctrine of the analogy of being which is disliked, almost as much as natural theology itself, by most of those theologians who reject natural theology. Personally, I do not think that the term general revelation has proved a very helpful one in contemporary theological discussion. I do not propose to use it at all in this book. In so far as I do use it, I prefer to reserve it for those occasions on which I discuss the question of whether or not any degree of divine revelation can be found in non-Christian religions. The term "natural theology," on the other hand, is one I shall employ when I am considering whether any degree of approximation to theological truths can conceivably be observed in the course of the development of general philosophy. In that way we can arrive at a rough-and-ready way—not, I am afraid, very profound or fundamental—of distinguishing between the two.

A definition of the word nature. As with many of the

great classic words of human thought, the word "nature," in the modern world, has become ambiguous. Now it seems to mean either everything in general or nothing in particular. "Everything in general" is nearly always, in practice, identical with "nothing in particular." Usually, the word nature is used as a collective noun to describe all the things that compose the non-human creation; it might have been better to have reserved some word such as *cosmos* for that purpose. Possibly the word nature can be made to include both the human and the nonhuman creation, in which case it becomes a collective noun identical with the noun creation (creation referring to the *creata,* the things created, and not to the activity of creating them). This may seem to be a more valid and a more Christian way of using the term nature. I prefer, however, to reserve the word *creation,* or the phrase *the realm of the creatures,* for this purpose.

In Greek philosophy and in classical Christian thought and theology, however, the nature of anything is its characteristic pattern of process. Thus, it is "in the nature of man" to grow out of childhood into an adult creature. *Nature* thus signifies the characteristic pattern of the type or species, its peculiar form or mode of growth and development.

From this point of view, we know there can be deviations from the natural as a result of many different combinations of circumstances. Thus, for example, man may deviate from the human *natura* through sin. The Fall means a catastrophic, primordial deviation from nature. Nature itself is both a descriptive and a normative term at one and the same time; it does describe a norm and it does purport, in the vast majority of cases, to describe a norm that is in fact observed.

But the essential meaning of the doctrine of the Fall consists in the statement that the peculiarity of the human norm (the human *natura*) is that, although it is the norm, it is not in fact always obeyed—perhaps because the human norm, unlike most natural norms, is not automatically or spontaneously observed but requires conscious, willing adhesion. It is part of the catastrophe in which man finds himself that he is not himself, that he is estranged from himself: being estranged from God, he is therefore estranged from both the origin and the end of his own being.

This takes us back to our first approach to natural theology. A natural theology is a kind of theology which is natural to man. This does not mean that it is the kind of theology which man nearly always or necessarily thinks; for, under sin and because of the Fall, man is not always natural, by any means. Nevertheless, this kind of theology is natural to man in the sense that the human mind approximates it in proportion as its thinking rises toward the ideal of complete rational integrity and undistorted humanity.

For the Christian philosopher the term "natural" carries with it another very important connotation. For him the realm of the natural, the whole created order, is the realm of that which can only be empirically known. The realm of the natural is, as the classical Christian philosophers and natural theologians say, contingent: it does not *have* to be; it simply *happens* to be. It is dependent upon the creative will of God, who quite conceivably might have created otherwise, or might even not have created at all.

16

Natural or created facts cannot be discovered and known by any process of purely rational analysis. They have to be observed and described; they can only be discovered in and through experience of them, in which they manifest and reveal themselves. To say this is to emphasize the closeness of the connection which exists between the Christian conception of nature, based on the Biblical doctrine of Creation, and the emergence of the natural sciences in and out of the expanding life of Christian civilization, as a revelation of its hitherto latent implications. This recognition that knowledge of natural facts cannot be obtained by purely rational analysis (*i.e.* that empirical knowledge is not *apriori*) will also be seen to have great significance for us in the later stages of our discussions in this book.

The Cosmological Argument

As I have said, for most people the norm of natural theology is the second of the four approaches, "an argument based on naturalistic premises." And this argument, classically called the cosmological or teleological argument, is any variant of the general idea, "because the world exists, God exists."

There are many forms of this argument, and it can be expressed very crudely, for example, as: "Somebody had to make everything else, so I suppose somebody had to make the world." (Conceivably, this is just permissible, occasionally, in the Sunday school class, and I think most Sunday School classes get it at some time or other!) But obviously the argument does not have to be in this crude form; it can be a mechanistic argument for a Supreme Mechanic, or a

17

technological argument for a Supreme Architect. In the works of quite recent writers such as Sir James Jeans and Sir Arthur Eddington, it has been a mathematician's argument for a Supreme Mathematician (and that is also the form which it assumed centuries ago in Plato's *Timaeus*). Or it can be, as in Whitehead, a metaphysician's argument for a final and ultimate creative principle that regulates the interplay between the potential and the actual.

There can also be aesthetic forms of the cosmological argument. This may on one hand consider reality as primarily a work of art and the nonhuman-creation as something closely analogous to the visual and plastic arts (the analogy being betrayed by the fundamental similarity that exists between our aesthetic response to nature as a spectacle and our aesthetic response to visual art as a spectacle); or, on the other hand, it may trace an analogy between the human life and works of drama and fiction, betrayed when we use some such phrase as "the drama of history." (Very often we find people who say that they prefer good history or biography to novels because they are even more extraordinary.) For example, in Dorothy Sayers' *The Mind of the Maker* and in other similar books we find such an aesthetic form of the cosmological argument.

Its Existential Form

There is also what I would call an existential form of the cosmological argument, going back at least to Augustine, and finding a very profound re-expression in the often sadly heretical philosophy of Johannes Scotus Erigena in the ninth century. In its existential form, the fundamental contingency (the dependence) of the real, as we know it, upon that which transcends it is discovered particularly and most vividly of all in man's experience of self-conscious existence.

I lay some stress on the analogy between the form of the argument, "because the world exists, God exists," and the existential argument, "because I exist and suffer and agonize and go through all that I do, and know myself to be dependent and contingent, therefore God exists," since I think it is true that a very considerable number of people in the twentieth century fail to see that what they call an existential approach to theology is fundamentally as naturalistic as Thomas Aquinas' cosmological approach to theology. In each case the Christian thinker is beginning with, and using as a bridge to his adumbration of the meaning of the Gospel and the Christian faith, a number of considerations drawn from man's experience of existing in the world.

The cosmological kind of natural theology may stress the world, and the existential kind of natural theology may stress human existence, but they have one basic postulate in common: they both claim, through their analysis of that phase of our experience with which they are preoccupied, to discover the fundamental "give-away" fact of the contingency of the real. A Thomist may look at the world and say, "Aha! The world is contingent!" An existentialist may look at himself within the world and say, "Aha! I am contingent, and I have a shrewd suspicion that other people are contingent, too!" But if the existentialist theologian adds, "How much profounder am I than the Thomist with his merely natural theology!" he is mistaken. He is using the word natural only in the sense of cosmic, but more accurately, as we have seen, nature includes both human existence and the cosmos. Or, alternatively, both man and the cosmos are characterized by their own specific natures.

We are now in a position to see the significance of at least some part of our brief digression on the meaning of nature. It indicates that the existentialist approach to theology, so fashionable among contemporary theologians, and above all among those contemporary theologians who make the greatest parade of rejecting all natural theology, is itself a form of natural theology. We only make the mistake of supposing that an existentialist theology is not natural theology, and is even opposed in spirit to natural theology, because we have formed the bad habit of using the word nature as a collective noun for all the subhuman things which compose the cosmos.

Once we understand the word nature properly, we see clearly enough that a theology or philosophy which takes for its point of departure man's self-conscious experience of his own existence is just as naturalistic in its premises as one which takes for its point of departure our observation and knowledge of the cosmos which environs us. There is much to be said for the view that this existentialist approach to theology is the form of natural theology most appropriate to the climate of opinion which predominates in the twentieth century, just as the cosmological approach found in Thomas Aquinas was the form of natural theology most appropriate to the climate of opinion in the thirteenth century. But this does not mean that any fundamental distinction can, or should be, drawn between them, still less that each is opposed to the other in its essential spirit.

We must always remember that natural theology is in some sense a missionary as well as a purely intellectual enterprise. Hence, the natural theologian must always be peculiarly sensitive to the climate or climates of opinion predominating in his own time. Thus, when we read the *Summa Contra Gentiles,* we must never lose sight of the fact that Thomas was a kind of missionary to the Aristotelians, traversing not physical distances in order to get to the other side of the globe, like the more familiar kind of missionary, but traveling vast metaphysical distances in order to get to the mind and speak to the condition of his students and colleagues.

Today many Christian theologians are similarly impressed with the rise and vogue of the many highly diverse forms of philosophy which we describe as existentialist, and they are right to see that even in its most radically antireligious form it has a deep significance for Christian thought. Nevertheless, they are wrong to assume that there is any fundamental departure in either the conclusions or the spirit of their thinking from that characteristic of Thomas and the cosmological theologians.

Inference and Revelation

We will postpone for the moment any consideration of the intellectual value of such arguments; but before closing this first chapter, I would like to reconsider briefly its first form: the doctrine of an inherent ordination of man, even

intellectually, toward God. I believe that it is at this point
that many of our difficulties and misunderstandings begin.
Hence, this is the point at which it is necessary, by a certain
amount of re-definition, to begin to clear up these misunderstandings.

"Both-and" or "Either-or"

Broadly speaking, when two beings thinking in the same
tradition (as, for example, two Christian theologians) differ
from each other there are always two possible explanations:
first, that they only think they differ with each other because
they do not quite understand each other. I believe that we
should always assume at first that this is what is happening.
At all events, I am sure it is the irenical Anglican way to
begin with such an assumption! The other possibility is that
they really do differ. But let us not acquiesce in that conclusion until we are driven to do so by stern ineluctable facts.
Let us start on the more hopeful assumption that something
can be done in the way of re-definition, re-explanation, and
re-thinking.

In some respects it does seem to me that the whole mind
and bent of Anglicanism is rather synthetic or Hegelian.
Many so-called dialectical theologians seem to delight in
multiplying "either-or" situations, by impaling the reader
on the horns of one dilemma after another. But the Anglican mind always dislikes arbitrary "either A or B" situations, and tends to say, "surely, we can have both A^1 and
B^1." I say both A^1 and B^1 and not both A and B because a
true synthesis does more than merely lump together its two
terms in a bare paradox. Instead, it transforms and enriches

the meaning of each term in the very process of reconciling it to the other. A true synthesis is neither a compromise nor a self-contradiction, but a profounder apprehension.

Kierkegaard criticized Hegel by saying that there are certain either-or situations in life which cannot be bridged or transcended in the Hegelian way. I do not doubt that Kierkegaard was right. But I think there is something to be said for assuming that we may be in a both-and situation first, and only reluctantly agreeing that we are in an either-or situation when we are ultimately constrained by the facts. That seems to me a very good form of intellectual procedure. When we leap to the either-or situation it is just possible that behind the severity of our judgment there lies a very real intellectual laziness, or possibly sometimes a very real intellectual uncharity.

On the other hand, in order to show that the laugh can sometimes be against the Anglican, we may remind ourselves of the story of the very, very modernist Anglican bishop who was asked whether or not he believed in God. He replied, "I dislike these hard and fast distinctions."

This suggests that there are certain ultimate limitations to the Anglican mode of intellectual procedure. It suggests also that Kierkegaard was right in the end. All I am proposing is that we should not assume that he was necessarily right at the beginning.

My own conviction is that in the realm of philosophy and theology—where honest and gifted and not seldom intellectually inspired men differ from one another and wrestle not against one another for the mastery, but with one another for the truth—both-and situations arise much more frequently than either-or situations, although it may well be that the latter, precisely because they are so rare, are, when we do meet with them, more profound and more fundamental to our whole way of life and thought.

If this is so, the proper rule of intellectual procedure should be always to begin by assuming that we are in a both-and situation until we are driven by the failure of a prolonged course of intellectual experiment to the conclusion that we are, in fact, in one of those either-or situations in which we have to state and hold our position without compromise. Either-or situations are more commonly met with in the realms of ethical action and decision than in that of pure, truth-seeking thought.

It is with this rule of procedure in mind that I want to turn once more to the contrast between intellectual inference and expectation on the one hand and the facts or events which verify such inferences and fulfil such expectations on the other. We have already glimpsed the possibility that the relationship between revelation and natural theology may be a relationship of this kind. If this is so, the two cannot be validly or fruitfully opposed to each other, because in fact they need each other. Just as inference cannot verify itself or fulfil its own expectations, so revelation cannot be fully understood or appropriated by man unless he is in a position to note which of his inferences it verifies and which of them it disproves; which of his expectations it fulfils and which of them it shows to be groundless. After all, the revelation of God does not come to us in a mental and spiritual vacuum. It is given to living, thinking men, and it has a dynamic relationship to their life and thought alike.

I shall speak of inference and the verification of inference in general terms, but the reader must have in mind that I do so because I regard these general considerations as vitally relevant to our present discussion. I believe that much of the controversy about the relationship of, and supposed antagonism between, reason and revelation can be resolved, and even seen not to arise, in terms of a better understanding of the relationship between inference and verification.

Experience may be said to have a revelatory character, because experience has a way of either verifying or failing to verify inference. Hence it partakes of the nature of revelation. I am using the word revelation broadly, meaning not religious revelation only, because we are surrounded by revelation at every moment. To meet and gradually come to know another human being is to watch him reveal himself. Similarly, sense experience is a form of revelation. The color of the walls of a room is revealed to us when we first enter and behold it. We know no way of calculating rationally what color the walls must be prior to or without entering the room.

I see no possibility of revelation being given except to rational beings, and I see no possibility of the exercise of reason except within some revelational context. Fundamentally, as I see it, the opposition between reason and revelation is similar to the attempt to oppose the left to the right, or the north to the south, or the east to the west, since the two terms involve each other. Rational thought is always thought about a revealed reality or datum, and a revealed reality or datum can have meaning only to an intellectual creature.

The Transcending of Inference

We should note, however, for it is the really important point, that although revelation—the event, the fact—may and sometimes does confirm inference, it never *merely* confirms inference; it always more than confirms inference. Take an example: the young wife, full of joy and trepidation and hope, goes to see her family doctor. He examines her and says, "My dear, you're going to have a baby." It is conceivable that he is wrong—although probably not if he's an experienced family doctor—but it's just conceivable that she has some kind of growth in the reproductive organs; and of course it's always conceivable that she will have a miscarriage. Still she is probably going to have a baby, and normally the event, the revealing event, will among other things verify the doctor's inference.

In another way, however, it will negate the inference, because she will not have *a* baby, she will have *the* baby, a very different thing! No mother that ever lived has had *a* baby—just a pale, tenuous something which verifies the doctor's inference and no more! The revelation always transcends the inference which points to it. The revelation is never identical with the inference, for the inference is always an idea, and the revelation is always a reality.

It seems to me that it is the failure to observe this that underlies a lot of talk about "the God of Aristotle" or "the

God of the Greeks" not being "the God of the Bible," or something of that kind. I really do not know what this means. There are not two Gods, presumably; and surely we should all agree that the cosmic functions of God in Aristotle, for example (no doubt in a vague, confused way which calls for a great deal of analysis and criticism and correction), are carried out by the God whom we worship as Biblical Christians. The mere fact that in a very different context, from a very different aspect, with a very different degree of intimacy, two people give very different accounts of the same person does not mean that they are really two distinct persons!

Sometimes under favorable circumstances, I draw money from my bank which is just around the corner from my home. Usually, out of habit I suppose, I go to the same teller. I can provide a description of him: he's a young man; with dark hair and a rather dark, swarthy skin; a pleasant manner; usually rather well turned out—nice tie, collar always very clean. He works swiftly but always accurately. He has never made a mistake, but then it would be very difficult to make a mistake as far as I am concerned. I should conclude, therefore, that he is a typical and efficient teller.

But suppose that instead of coming to me, the inquirer went to the young man's wife. I wonder what sort of picture he would get from her. I do not know, of course, but he may (I hope he would) get a picture of a loving husband, a very affectionate and dutiful father—possibly a churchwarden at the local church or a secretary of an amateur dramatic group. There are all sorts of possibilities, and, of course, the more she is willing to reveal her intimate experience of life with him, the more rounded the picture will be of, shall we say, a true-hearted, generous, chivalrous man: good neighbor, good husband, good father, and so on.

Will it be valid, then, for the inquirer to say, "Look, we've got two men here! This affectionate father has nothing to do with the soulless efficiency machine." Will he therefore have two men or will either informant necessarily have lied? I think not. We must say at once that because one picture is so much fuller, warmer, more intimate, more profound, it does not necessarily mean that there is no truth at all in the other picture.

I am using this as an illustration of the relationship between inference and revelation; revelation will do more than verify the inference, even in the most favorable circumstances. It will transcend inference to some extent, and to some extent confound inference. I too may very well be confounded if I talk to the teller's wife. I may admit surprise and ask, "Do you mean to say that this man with his slick counting, this man who, when I see him, seems to live for money and taps out figures on his counting machine with such impersonal efficiency—do you really mean to say that he is a romantic lover who moves you to your very depths?" That quick little fellow, who seems almost like a living mathematical table, must now be imagined in another mood as capable of sweeping the young woman off her feet! I may add, "I'm utterly dumbfounded to hear it! It's completely outside my expectations."

Thus it is that revelation may and does confound as well as verify inference. But the inference is not invalid because it is confounded and transcended; it is indeed, in its own degree, verified. Of course, not all inferences are verified, only some. But it is enough for the natural theologian, looking at the thoughts and the hopes and the fears of a non-Christian world, to find at least some inferences which he can verify, even though he must then proceed to transcend and confound them with the tremendous glory of the whole gospel.

Greek and Hebrew

I have already remarked that the relationship of the gospel to philosophy is in many ways akin or parallel to its relationship to Hebrew prophecy. There also we see events at the same time fulfilling and transcending, transcending to the point of confounding, previous outlooks and expectations. Paul noted this parallelism in the first chapter of his first Epistle to the Corinthians when he remarked that the preaching of the gospel is "to the Jews a stumbling block; to the Greeks foolishness." This passage is sometimes appealed to by those theologians who make a particular point of stressing the Hebraic character of the Christian faith. Such writers often delight in elaborating a view which interprets the Greek outlook as the dialectical antithesis of the Hebrew mentality. They insist that any influence of Greek thought on the development of Christian theology must necessarily have been a corrupting one, estranging it from its own sources.

In fact, however, Paul's words assert both an analogy between the two and their relationship to the Christian gospel. Neither Hebrew religion nor Greek philosophy can receive the gospel as long as either of them regards itself as a closed and wholly satisfactory system. In other words, there were Hebrew as well as Greek reasons for refusing to accept the gospel. We may note in passing that the Christian Church has had to wrestle in its history with Judaizing as well as Hellenizing heresies and distortions of the gospel and that, on the whole, in the New Testament period, as perhaps in the epoch of Protestant religion and theology, the former danger presented the greater menace of the two. It is only if and when Hebrew religion and the kind of philosophy we have inherited from the Greeks are open systems, ready to receive new facts and experiences and ready to criticize their past insights and achievements in the light of them, that either can enter into the context of Christian faith and enrich the life of the Church with the values and spiritual and intellectual skills which each richly possesses. The controversy among modern theologians about the respective values of the Greek and Hebrew contributions to Christian theology is a barren and misleading one. It is only when men differ from each other in the same medium and in relation to the same questions that their differences commit them to lifelong opposition. It is precisely because the differences between the Greek and Hebrew outlooks were so great and fundamental that it was possible for them to ally themselves with each other and complement each other in the life and thought of the early Church, with such astonishing fruitfulness and epoch-making consequences.

Of course, Greek thought and Hebrew religion came into contact with each other and mutually influenced each other to a certain extent before the period of the Christian dispensation began, and to some extent they continued to do so, for example, in Philo and Hellenistic-Judaism and in the Jewish scholasticism of Maimonides a thousand years later, outside the limits of Christianity altogether. But it was in the life and thought of the early Church that there took place the most profound and important confrontation of the Hebrew and the Greek, and it was in that context that there was hammered out the mighty synthesis which it is still possible, indeed I should say necessary, for the Christian to regard and interpret as one of the great providential acts of God in human history.

Two Major Problems

Out of the chief types of natural theology, which I have attempted to describe very briefly, there arise two major problems. Particularly from the first, second, and third of the four forms of natural theology, which I described briefly, there arises the fundamental problem: in what sense, if any, may we validly suppose, believe, and say that some vestige of the image of God in man survives the catastrophe of the Fall? In what sense, also, if any, is some kind of analogy of being (*analogia entis,* as the theologians call it) permissible and possible in the thought of fallen man?

This is a problem indeed, but the other problem is an even greater one. From the third and fourth types of natural theology, in particular, there arises the whole question of the scope of theology as a science: can we rest content with a methodological conception of theology which makes it one specialism among many, a particular form of intellectual application and discipline which studies a certain selection of religious and Christian data connected with the original and basic deposit of faith? Very roughly, we may say that theology as a specialism studies the Bible, the history of the Church, and to a rather smaller extent the classic sub-Biblical documents which have appeared and achieved some kind of importance and vogue in Church history, *e.g.*, liturgies and the writings of such great classical theologians as Augustine, Aquinas, Luther, Calvin, and so on.

Shall we rest content with the methodological concept of theology as a specialism or shall we be driven in our modern world, with the tremendous and thrilling revival of theological studies and theological acumen which the twentieth century has witnessed, to an attempt to restate something like the medieval doctrine of a science which is not just *a* science but in some real sense the queen of the sciences—one in which we find the clue to the meaning and interpretation of all the other sciences.

The first of these two problems is of such immediate relevance at this stage of our discussion that we shall turn to it in the next chapter. The second problem, however, we shall for the moment leave on one side, returning to it at a later stage.

CHAPTER TWO

THE IMAGE OF GOD IN FALLEN MAN

The first of our two major problems (whether vestiges of the image of God have survived in fallen man) perhaps arises from what has been said far more obviously than the second. Many contemporary theologians, particularly in Europe, might well point out (in almost as many ways as there are theologians) that in all that we have said so far about some kind of Godward intellectual process of which the premises are naturalistic, the fact of the Fall and the consequences of the Fall for human knowledge and for what we call man's noetic capacities are overlooked. A great deal of authority can be cited from the central traditions of the Christian Church (not all of it necessarily from the great reformers—some also from the scholastics and from the fathers) for holding that the possibility of an intellectual movement toward God would have existed had man not fallen, but cannot be held to exist now that man has fallen.

Calvin's Epistemological Position

I am not at all sure whether all this authority can be quoted for some of the extreme radical positions which are adopted today. As I understand Calvin, for example, his real point is not so much that natural theology as conceived by some of his predecessors is impossible but rather that, because man is fallen and the human intellect is distorted and has become to a very large extent the instrument of his sin, the consequences of natural theology are idolatrous. It leads him to worship, not the living God of the Biblical revelation, but an intellectualized, private God of his own: his creature rather than his Creator.

I will not attempt to substantiate this interpretation of Calvin here, because the task would take me beyond the limits of this book. But I will ask the reader to accept this view as a *prima facie* possible interpretation of much that Calvin had to say; and I hasten to add that fundamentally I am in agreement with such a thesis, though there are certain qualifications which I propose to make. Somebody remarked that about a hundred years ago a certain American professor of theology is alleged to have said, "Of course, I wouldn't claim that Calvin is infallible; I will merely say that I have never found him to be wrong." With humility, I must admit that I could repeat those words without some exaggeration of my real feelings. Nevertheless, on any showing, and whatever one's situation or standpoint in Christendom, Calvin is one of the great theologians. His work and witness must be taken into account with reverence and consideration.

The Confusion Between Finitude and Sin

In much of the reformed theology since Calvin's day, particularly during the last century and a half (roughly since the publication of the first of Kant's three *Critiques*) there has grown up a position which appears to resemble Calvin's, but actually is not the same thing at all. Again, as I understand it, Calvin's position is that the trouble with human reasoning is that it always functions within a context of sin; whereas a very considerable amount of modern reformed theology, which has taken copious draughts of the critical epistemology of Immanuel Kant and his successors, says in effect that the trouble with human reasoning is not so much that man is a sinner as that man is finite.

Clearly, these are two very different statements. If the trouble with human reasoning is that man is a sinner, then indeed the fundamental maladies of human reasoning are in a real and profound sense accidental to his essential being, and therefore tragic. To say that man is a sinner is to set man in the category of tragedy. But to say that the trouble with human reasoning is that man is man (which is what the critical philosophers really say when they teach that it is the finitude of man's being which restricts his rational powers) is not to put man in the category of the tragic; it is to put man in the category of the unfortunate, a very different category indeed.

The Critical Philosophy

It has become more and more clear that the critical philosophy is widely regarded as the philosophical ally or even philosophical propaedeutic to theology, and that it plays, and has played, for a considerable number of reformed theologians, both of the Lutheran and Calvinist persuasions during the nineteenth and twentieth centuries, a role similar to that which Thomism plays in so much contemporary Roman Catholic theology.

It is an added paradox that the Ritschlians, for example, and whole generations of antimetaphysical German theologians really supposed that they had gotten rid of metaphysics simply because they had swallowed Kant's metaphysics! In other words, I wish to suggest that certain imperfections and prejudices and characteristic blindnesses which we find in a good deal of nineteenth and twentieth century reformation theology are not due to the Reformation but to Immanuel Kant, as well as to the confusion between finitude and sin.

This is not meant as a full-blast attack on that very great man, Immanuel Kant. It might have been more just if I had said the Kantians, or merely the critical philosophers and epistemologists, including, of course, the positivists. The trouble is that the only work so many people know of Immanuel Kant is the first *Critique*, and that turns them into positivists. Then we come to a second group who know both the first and the second *Critiques*, and that turns them into antimetaphysical existentialists. Then, very rarely, there are those who also know the third *Critique*, and I think that makes them wonder very much about some of the things they read in the first and second *Critiques!* But by the Kantians I mean primarily the people who, so to speak, sold their all in order to buy the first *Critique*, under the illusion that this is the pearl of great price; and this in effect means that they are antimetaphysical positivists.

The essential procedure of all antimetaphysical positivists is to show, by an elaborate argument which purports to be an inspection of our rational powers by our rational powers (or, if we prefer it, a self-inspection of our rational powers) that reality is divided into a knowable and an unknowable part, phase, aspect (whatever word we choose will be somewhat confusing and difficult). Thus, the mind of man is forever restricted to a certain area of reality which may be called the world of phenomena, or the public world of natural science, or whatever we choose. The rest of reality is the world of noumena or metaphysics, and this is declared to be unknowable.

For a certain kind of theologian, you can see how this seems to fit beautifully the requirements of a revelational, Biblical theology. It means that the proper work of reason is to be found in the natural sciences, and possibly in literary and historical criticism and activities, but that, so far as ultimate (or what we used to call metaphysical) truths are concerned, we are, and we must remain, verily and indeed babes unborn. Therefore, philosophy has demonstrated the emptiness of a niche which only revelation can fill. (There are many different ways of putting this argument, and for this reason I am schematizing it in a relatively simple form that we can grasp easily and apprehend.)

Can a Man Know Anything Utterly?

First of all I want to argue that we can have no conceivable ground or warrant for supposing the existence of that which is in principle unknowable, as distinct from that which is in fact unknown. By definition we can have no experience which suggests the existence of such a thing; and clearly, by definition, we can have no knowledge of it whatsoever.

Of course, it is true that man can know, or rather seem to himself to know, realities which do not exist, or harbor in his mind incorrect beliefs about realities which do exist. That is, man can be deceived and cherish illusions. Men have believed that the earth is flat, and some children suppose for a time that the moon is made of green cheese and is inhabited by one solitary resident. But the problem of human error cannot be resolved, the fact of human error cannot be interpreted, by the simple expedient of supposing that there is some sphere of thought and research in which error is inevitable and then contrasting it with some other sphere in which error is either impossible or at least avoidable. In whatever sphere men think and do research, error is possible; in no such sphere is it inevitable.

Again, men can imaginatively compose for themselves meaningless or nonsense notions by devising incompatible arrangements of words like "a round square" or "a green conception." It is better to describe such notions as nonsense rather than meaningless, for it is only because we know the meaning of the phrases that we see them to be nonsense. The term meaningless has become a popular one in recent and contemporary philosophy, but its vogue is unfortunate. No matter how we define meaninglessness, it remains true that we can only describe a statement or an idea as meaningless if we are in a position to perceive its meaning.

The disease of language, the propensity of savage or sophisticated man to indulge in mere words that mean and point to nothing beyond themselves, is indeed a reality and a real problem for philosophy, but again we cannot deal with this problem by the over-simple method, characteristic particularly of the logical positivists, of laying it down that in some one sphere of thought and research all statements are necessarily meaningless. After all, no sphere of thought and research is immune from the effects of this particular disease.

Thus, human thought is always and everywhere in danger of falling into nonsense or meaninglessness, subject to fits of mere verbalization. But the positivists are greatly mistaken if they suppose that they can vanquish such dangers merely by placing a veto on all future indulgence in metaphysical speculation or by any arbitrary splitting of reality into knowable and unknowable phases or departments. Such a method will avail neither to banish the nonsense from the human mind nor to lead us to a right interpretation of the intellectual handicap inherent in our finitude.

My main charge against the critical and positivist philosophers is that they rightly perceive the finitude of man but misinterpret it. They say in effect, "The mark of the finitude of man is that there are a lot of things which in principle he cannot know." It seems to me much more profoundly true that the real mark of the finitude of the human intellect is that there is *nothing* which man can *utterly* know. The moment they define an unknowable part of reality, which is useless for us to bother about, there always is the suggestion that there is a knowable part which we can really know through and through.

In my opinion, this second suggestion is as unwarrantable as the first suggestion, and even more dangerous and intellectually misleading. Nearly always, the critical philosophy begins by being very humble about the human intellect and says, "It's no good our thinking about all these metaphysical questions because they exceed our rational powers," but it almost always ends by being unwarrantably dogmatic and complacent about that which it supposes we can know. For sheer contemporary dogmaticism, commend me to the logical positivists! They compensate themselves for the vast intellectual and metaphysical sacrifices they have made, the tremendous deed of abdication which they have signed in the name of humanity, by insisting that the little bit that is left is utterly and completely theirs: "Here, in this sphere, you can still dream your dreams of grandeur and glory and intellectual mastery!" In other words, it is a pseudo-humility when a man irresponsibly resigns a kingdom in order to become the autocrat of a cabbage patch.

On the contrary, what we really do know and what we have some warrant in experience for saying, is that all the realities of which we are aware are realities which we cannot entirely contain within our intellect; that whenever man has to do with reality, he cannot know it exhaustively, not even the simplest reality. Hence, he has to invent the various shortcuts to knowledge: for example, all the forms of

40

scientific knowledge which employ a generalizing, pigeon-hole method. This achieves knowledge by subsuming particulars under generalizations.

Take the phenomena of swans. I do not know how many swans there are in the world or how many swans there have been or how many swans there will be, but I do know that a complete list of all the possible general propositions about swans that it is possible to frame will not tell us all the truth about any one swan, let alone all the other swans. Even the finite thing has an infinity of potentially true propositions which may be made about it. The real mark of the finitude of the human mind is that no matter what reality it grasps and wrestles with, in some way the reality always escapes. This to me is the real significance of what some people call "the infinite regress," what Kant called "the antinomy," and, fundamentally, what Kierkegaard called "the paradox." The infinite regress, to my mind, is the sign that we are in touch with reality.

I first met the infinite regress when I was a very little boy. We used to eat a breakfast cereal, which I still see in the shops, called Post Toasties. In those days the box was most fascinating. It contained the picture of a little girl with long hair kneeling in front of a fire. Beside her was a box of Post Toasties, and on that box was a little girl with long hair, beside a fire, and near her was a box of Post Toasties! The artist had given up the ghost quite early, because that third box of Post Toasties had just a little squiggle on it. I was about four or five years old and pointed out to my father that really this never ended, it went on and on, box of Post Toasties, box of Post Toasties, box of Post Toasties, forever.

41

The artist could stop but the philosopher could not! My father replied, "Yes, my boy, but perhaps one day you will think that everything is like that fundamentally." Always, what we are left with is the knowledge that there is more to know. We push on and push on and push on, and we never get to the bottom of reality. The mind of man can never contain all of any reality, not even a box of Post Toasties.

The Corruption of Man's Situation

It seems to me this is the characteristic mark of the finitude of the human intellect: that *there is nothing which is utterly knowable,* not that there are a lot of things which are in principle unknowable. The doctrine that some things are in principle unknowable (the doctrine, that is, that the human intellect is not made for reality and not oriented toward it) seems to me to be identified with the doctrine of the Fall only by confusion. It is not the finitude of the human intellect which bedevils our thinking; it is the corruption and corruptibility of the human social situation, the psychological context within which that thinking is conducted.

In this way, although we may be forced to differ with a good many contemporary reformation theologians, we are actually getting closer to what *the* great reformation theologian really believed and taught. He did not confuse sin and finitude as certain contemporary theologians are inclined to do. Sometimes, as I read these modern theologians, I do not know whether according to them the trouble is that man is sinner or that man is man; and I do not know whether they confuse man's sin with his humanity, but I do know what they ought to mean. They ought to mean that the trouble is that man is sinner, and not at all that man is man.

In other words, it can be no part of our case or belief or argument that man is cut off by nature from reality. Reality must always exceed and transcend man's powers, but I personally agree with Duns Scotus that the intellect is by nature so flexible, so adaptable, and so resourceful that no reality is in principle outside its apprehension, though, because man's intellect is finite, every real thing is in principle outside the grasp of its comprehension, even our own being.

If this is true, we can retrace our steps once more, because now our problem is not the problem of how man can have a natural theology as a finite being, because a natural theology surely must deal with infinitely high matters beyond the power of the human intellect; now the real problem is: what is the effect of sin upon thought? First, however, I ought to summarize my reasons for rejecting any belief about the Fall that regards it as totally destroying both the image of God in man and man's capacity to perceive certain analogies between reality and the divine.

The ANALOGIA ENTIS

Barth rejects what he calls the *analogia entis* (the analogy of being), dismissing it as the characteristically Roman Catholic doctrine. (I am not convinced that this is in fact *the* characteristically Roman Catholic doctrine, but I have no doubt at all that most Roman Catholics believe in it.) Barth substitutes what he calls the *analogia fidei* (the analogy of faith); but I do not think his doctrine really meets, explains, those analogies between reality and the divine which are most familiar to us: the New Testament parables.

For example, a certain woman lost half a dollar, and she sweeps under every bit of furniture until she finds it, despite the fact that there are a dozen dollars in her purse. We do not add to the effect if we say, "A certain *Christian* woman lost half a dollar," and "in faith she sweeps." She does not do it in faith; she does it just because she is human. That is where the analogy is drawn. To say "A certain *believing* father had two sons" does not add anything to the parable; the parable simply gives us a human father, not a father who acts as he does in faith, but a father who acts as he does because he is a father. There is no doubt in my mind, as I look at the parables, that this is what the theologians mean by the *analogia entis*.

Sometimes we have the *analogia entis* in its, so to speak, existential phase, as "A certain man had two sons"; and the analogy is drawn in terms of the relationship of the father to his sons. But sometimes, as for example where the analogy is drawn from certain happenings within the life of nature, it has a cosmic basis. The nature parables are not parables of slow growth, but rather parables of secret growth and of an extremely surprising harvest. They are eschatological parables drawn from the life of nature. Here is this tiny piece of matter called a mustard seed, that a breath can blow away, and yet a huge plant comes out of it. It is a secret and above all an extraordinarily surprising process, so quick, so sudden, so complete a transformation. This is certainly the *analogia entis*. We must remember that the parables are not used first of all in the instruction of what we may call the faithful. They are expounded and interpreted later to the inner group of disciples. They are first used as forms of communication with all and sundry, with such human beings as happen to be present.

The Survival of the IMAGO DEI

Would such an analogical process as we have just looked at be possible in a world in which the *imago* had been entirely destroyed by the Fall, so that the *humanum* (the whole life of humanity) could no longer be said to exhibit any vestiges at all of the image of God? To my mind, it would be difficult to conceive how such a process could possibly take place. The parables imply some kind of vestige of the image, and I take it that by saying, "man is in the image of God," and by using the phrase, *imago Dei*, we mean that the life of man presents us with the possibility of deducing valid theological analogies.

The doctrine that man is made in the image of God is present in the Old Testament, although rarely referred to. We cannot determine the comparative importance of a Biblical notion simply by counting the number of occasions on which Scripture explicitly refers to it; on the contrary, its importance is manifested in the extent to which other passages in Scripture presuppose it without any explicit reference whatever. (This is one of the reasons why a merely verbal and literary exegetical treatment of Scripture is insufficient. The interpretation of the Bible must always be a theological as well as a literary activity.)

In the New Testament it is Jesus Christ, the God-man, rather than merely man, who presents the image of God.

45

Man has to be remade in the image of God in and by and through the redemptive forces let loose among men by the eternal Image who is also the eternal Word of God. (The most exhaustive list of possible prepositions will not, of course, do justice to the subtle reality and many-sidedness of the spiritual processes of which the New Testament speaks.)

Perhaps there is some danger in the simple, unsophisticated statement that man is made in the image of God. This too easily suggests that everything which enters into the present human reality in some sense reflects the Divine Being, and there can be little doubt that the doctrine of the image often meant for the Hebrew religious consciousness in Old Testament times that God has a body, the outlines of which are mirrored or reflected in the human body. It is better to stress the preposition and say that man is made *in* the image of God, or if we prefer it, to say that man contains the image or presents or reflects certain aspects of the image.

Thus, when I look in a mirror, the mirror reflects my face but not the back of my head; and although a part of my image is reflected in the mirror, it is not true to say that the whole mirror is my image. To me it seems impossible to proclaim either that the whole reality of man is the image of God or that the whole reality of God is reflected in such an image of Him as the human reality presents. I prefer to say that certain peak aspects of the human being—rationality, freedom, capacity for love, personality or uniqueness, spirituality, a need and craving for God, a native orientation of mind in a Godward direction, a sense of humor—do indeed

46

reflect certain aspects of the Divine Being. As a result there remains in human life, even fallen human life, the possibility of detecting and elaborating valid analogies by means of which we can approach and grow in a knowledge and understanding of God. It is this possibility that enabled Christ to utter the New Testament parables, and it is this possibility that enables us to devise for ourselves similar means of religious communication in the contemporary world.

The image is that from which we can draw a valid analogy which will give some sort of clue to, or information about, that which the image reflects. Where there is an image there is the possibility of analogy, though it may often be little more than a possibility, and only very rarely an actuality. In this sense, it seems to me that we must hold to the belief that we may properly speak of the survival of some vestige of the image of God in man despite the catastrophe of the Fall.

Again, I do not think that any of the basic religious values which those who go further and deny the possibility of any such survival at all wish to uphold are necessarily abandoned in what I have said. These basic religious values are man's complete dependence upon the power and mercy of God. Certainly, we all wish to assert these values. Every Christian must agree that man is not only finite and contingent and dependent upon the power of God, but also a sinner dependent utterly upon the mercy and the grace of God. These values must be upheld by any Christian who proposes to preach the gospel; for if they are not true, there is no point in preaching any gospel, because man would not need one. He might need a little bracing and exhortation now and then (a little "uplift" as it is called), but he would not need a gospel. Clearly, any man who proposes to preach a gospel must hold this kind of belief about the human predicament and about man's relation to God.

But it has never seemed to me that in order to maintain this position, we need go to the length of denying any kind of survival whatsoever of the image in fallen man. In other words, to say that all men are sinners and dependent upon God's mercy does not seem to me to imply or require a belief in the total disappearance of the image and of all vestiges of God's original purpose and norms for men as a result of the catastrophe of the Fall.

On the contrary, especially if we are thinking in terms of the major and central Calvinistic belief in the power of God, there is a very real difficulty about conceiving the Fall as total. To say that the Fall has entirely obliterated all vestiges of the image of God in man is surely to attribute an immense potentiality to sin—a potentiality which it is very difficult for us to attribute to any activity of the finite and the human, even if we add the sin of the fallen angels to the sin of man. I remember a profound phrase from, I think, the Authorized Version of the Book of Ecclesiastes (whose subsequent fate in many revisions I have forborne to trace, for I like it so very much as it is): "Whatsoever God doeth, he doeth it for ever."

Surely, we must believe that there is still some sense in which the "divinity shapes our ends, roughhew them how we will," that the stamp of God's work and the reality of God's purpose is still upon us, despite our sin.

The Wounding of Man

Indeed, would the tragedy of man be so tragic if his Fall were total? Surely the tragedy of human existence as we know it lies precisely in the way in which it brings conflict and deformation into the very length and breadth and depth of our human being. A total Fall, a complete corruption, might at least have spared us that, for it is not our experience that the conflict is known only in the mind of the converted man who still belongs to a fallen world, who is still tempted and still sins. We find, on the contrary, crowding in upon us every day, evidence of the immense destructive scale and scope of the conflict in every man, wherever he may be. In other words, a picture of man deeply and gravely wounded by the Fall, desperately ill as a consequence of the Fall, and yet still in some sense man, fits the actual situation of being a fallen human being, and our existential experience of that predicament, very much better than any doctrine of total Fall.

Sometimes I wonder (though I forbear to press this) whether in this doctrine of the titanic character of human sin there is not a kind of strange, inverted humanism. I wonder whether, in renouncing forever the illusions of inherent righteousness—the illusion that man is a being who is in process of evolving through time toward an ultimate perfection—there is not a tendency to say in effect, "Well, no doubt man was a bit of a failure in the part of the saint, but see how he plays the sinner! What an heroic sinner he can be, and how boldly he wrestles against God!" In this tremendous stress upon the way in which the Fall has undone man and, according to some theologians, obliterated every vestige of the image in man and destroyed in him every capacity to trace in himself or in his surroundings any kind of analogy to the being of the Creator, I do sometimes sense and detect this kind of "humanism turned upside down." Here the glory of man turns out to be a bestiality which, at least, is a tribute to the power of his sin to thwart the purpose of his Maker.

A Verification of the Effect of Sin

I have suggested that we are wisest and closest to human experience (including our evangelical experience of the Gospel as we find it in Scripture) if we do not regard the Fall of man as quite total, and if we see in man, as we know him and as we *are* him, some surviving vestiges of the image of God and some clue to the being and character of God. These, we have admitted, are not enough to get man very far if left to himself, because of the distorted character of his sinful thinking.

The stress on the distorting pressure of sin upon reason is the part of the Calvinist tradition with which I want to agree very strongly, without any critical reservations at all. Of course, it is not peculiar to the Calvinist tradition. Thomas Aquinas knew about it, and so, indeed, did Augustine. But, they were perhaps prone at times, a little airily, to assume that complete intellectual integrity (a complete swaying and guiding of the reason of man in and by the light of the reasoning of God) is a more frequent event in human history and a moral quality more easy to come by than it really is.

In the modern world we know a good deal more about the wounding of human intellectual integrity by the sin and selfishness of man, because we have had at least two major scientific theories (one from sociology and one from psychology) which in a way have verified what we may call "the theological hypothesis." These are: first, the theory of the ideology—the theory of the distorting pressure of our group interests upon our thought. Second, the theory of the rationalization—the theory of the way in which our complexes and our suppressed and unconscious wishes (and sometimes our conscious wishes) influence the direction and current of our thought, and often overthrow and confound our intellectual integrity.

The theory of the ideology was first stated by Marx, and the theory of the rationalization by Freud. That does not mean that these theories were perfectly stated by either of these writers. Quite clearly they were not. To both men, however, credit must be given for discovering new ideas of the utmost importance. Both of them, although perhaps unwittingly, are really studying the ways in which the Fall and human sin dominate human thought and confound the reason. We now know that a great deal of what supposes itself to be, and is often supposed to be, genuine ratiocination (true honest thinking) is in fact either ideology or rationalization or some combination of both. In other words, as so often happens, and as we should like to see happening more and more (indeed Christian thinkers must be continually conducting intellectual experiments with the object of adding to the known instances of this important process), the theological dogma is turned into a sociological or psycho-

51

logical hypothesis and verified by subsequent sociological or psychological thought and research.

We ought not to be disturbed by these truths. I can never understand why Christians are sometimes horrified by revelations of this kind. For example, when I meet with Christians who are scandalized by the Freudian uncovering of the seamy side of the unconscious, or perhaps by the rather dubious calculations of Mr. Kinsey, I am inclined to say at once, "But, my dear fellow, why are you surprised? I thought you believed in the Fall. The man who believes in the Fall should at least be unshockable!" It is indeed an odd paradox if a man says he believes in the Fall of man yet is shocked at anything human. Let us leave it to the romantic humanists to be shocked at these revelations. Being shocked at this kind of thing is no part of our game, so to speak.

It is strange that so many people who proclaim that they accept the orthodox belief in original sin are so little aware of the meaning and implications of their own theology that they are continually surprised and scandalized by the spectacle of the visible sins of their neighbors. After all, the visible sins are no more than the outward manifestation of the underlying sinfulness, and the orthodox Christian should not be particularly shocked or surprised by their evidence.

Similarly, as we come to know more about the sins and sinfulness concealed in the lower depths of the human mind, the Christian should accept this new knowledge as a further confirmation of his own theological beliefs, neither surprising nor shocking, but precisely what his theology should lead him to expect. The laconic President Coolidge's Baptist preacher was described as being against sin. But more pro-

foundly understood, however, the essentially Christian attitude is against sinfulness rather than against sin, against the
underlying causal malady rather than against the outward
consequences and symptoms, and in no circumstances whatsoever against the sinner.

One of the troubles with many of the morally censorious
Christians, who know not of what theological spirit they
are, is that they are not merely shocked and scandalized by
the spectacle of real sins, but they are shocked and scandalized by the spectacle of sins which they have, so to speak, invented for themselves by their own puritanical prohibitions.
Some Christians believe it is sinful to dance, drink a glass of
wine or beer, attend a theater, or play a game of cards. An
earnest evangelical character in a contemporary play re-
marks, "Coffee is so nice. I can't understand why it isn't
a sin." But there are groups of Christians for whom even
drinking coffee is a sin. The odd thing is that such Christians are almost always pious evangelical sectarians who
delight to proclaim that the Bible and the Bible alone provides them with their sole authority and rule of life.

Where in Holy Scripture, we may ask, can we find the
smallest warrant for the puritanical habit of inventing new
and more categories of sin? Surely, the Puritan's hatred of
joy, his unseemly delight in a disapproval of his neighbors,
has nothing whatever to do with Biblical Christianity. The
trouble with this puritanical misunderstanding and abuse
of Christian doctrine is that it tends to make the Church's
theology of original sinfulness and actual sin ridiculous in
theory and nauseating in practice. There are quite enough
real sins without our inventing new ones. In any case, the

53

visible sins are not the heart of the matter. What God is dealing with in and through the Gospel is primarily the profoundly submerged sinfulness inherent in man's present fallen condition. It is precisely because this is true that a scrupulously observant morality, as the Christian preacher has to proclaim so insistently and so often, is not enough.

No doubt a scrupulously observant morality can deal fairly efficiently with most of the sins most of the time, but it cannot even begin to touch the inward and underlying sinfulness. Perservering morality is not enough; man has to be redeemed and re-created. If this is so, any and every kind of new knowledge that reveals and brings home to us the depth and extent of the malady which besets our being should be warmly welcomed by the Christian mind.

Man, as psychoanalysis reveals him, is certainly not a being whose problem can be solved by rigorous prohibitions. Indeed, despite the philosophical and theological confusions which cloud the counsels of so many psychoanalysts, they have on the whole been right to protest against the folly and futility of attempting to solve deep-seated human problems and tensions by the mere mechanism of repression. They are not merely pragmatically right, but they are also theologically right, more profoundly Christian than the Puritans against whose regime they protested. The God who reveals Himself in Jesus Christ is not a repressor who shuts man up in a moral reformatory, but a Saviour who sets man free.

Ideology as Sin

The aim of this digression has been to show how the theories of the ideology and the rationalization, and the new and deeper dimensions of sinfulness which they have revealed, may be interpreted as a very welcome and very real verification of a profound theological hypothesis about man, and the effect of his sinfulness on the whole course of his life and thought. But, let us notice this with some care: ideology and the rationalization are processes which can distort and poison not only our philosophical and metaphysical thinking, not only our thinking in the sphere of natural theology, but equally, let us admit it, our thinking in any sphere whatsoever, including the sphere of what we may call revelational or Biblical and dogmatic theology.

For example, about two years ago I was at a conference in Switzerland where we met many theologians whose native tongue was German. One of the most distinguished of these (whose name would be recognized at once if I mentioned it: a man who has labored long to eliminate from theological thinking every external social or secular pressure and interest) remarked at the end of the meeting, in his loudest prophetic tones (I say prophetic because he is normally inclined to say *no* to almost everything and everybody):

"The great burning reality about which God cares in this present time is the reunification of Germany."

Let me remind you that if one of us had said, "The great thing in God's eyes at the moment is the Atlantic community" or "the Americo-British alliance" or something of the kind, how he would have pounced on us! With what prophetic fury he would have denounced us and rent us and left us without a rag of self-respect to our names. Yet, the reunification of Germany was for him in quite a different category.

Thus, all of us can be caught. All forms of human thinking can be affected by ideological motives. Let me use an illustration from another sphere altogether. We observe the same process in the development of Marxist criticism and self-criticism. Obviously, the first difficulty for the Marxist theory of the ideology is the question: "Is Marxism itself an ideology?" At first sight it may appear that Marxism is merely the ideology of the revolutionary proletariat, but the Marxists can never admit this. For them, Marxism is not ideology. Marxism is a science, and science is never ideological (at least, so they supposed at first). Then the problem arises: how and in what sense is Marxism a science? And, in what way must we re-define the word *science* in order to make it clear that Marxism is science, whereas other and fundamentally kindred political and social doctrines are not science.

This is not easy, but at least it gives us a new dogma —science is non-ideological. Science is the one sphere of thought that is immune from all ideological distortion. But what happens in Marxism in the twentieth century? Here, we find the physical scientists suddenly accused and purged because of bourgeois deviations into a pseudo-scientific idealism. Then, the biologists and the economists are purged for more or less the same reason. Apparently, science can be ideological after all. Thus, the original reason for holding that Marxism itself is not ideology falls to the ground.

There is a witty passage in Arthur Koestler's novel, *The Age of Longing*, which charmingly satirizes the consequences of the Soviet discovery that science, like anything else, is subject to ideological pressures. He writes:

56

In fact, Lord Edwards in his young days had made an original contribution to Lemaitre's theory of the expanding universe. But shortly afterwards the Central Committee of the Commonwealth decreed that the universe was not expanding, and that the whole theory was a fabrication of bourgeois scientists reflecting the imperialist drive for the conquest of new markets.

The "hyenas of expansionist cosmology" were duly purged and Edwards, though he lived safely in England and had nothing to fear, published a book in which he proved that the universe was in peaceful equilibrium, without ever intending to expand. After the second world war, when the Commonwealth began to incorporate the neighboring republics and to spread its frontiers towards East and West, the Central Committee decided that the universe was expanding after all, and that the theory of a static universe was a fabrication of bourgeois science, reflecting the stagnant decay of capitalist economy. After some twenty million factory workers and collective farmers had sent in resolutions calling for death to the "stagnationist vermin," Edwards published another book proving that the universe was indeed expanding, had always been expanding and would go on expanding *ad infinitum.*[1]

By the Grace of God

There is no form of human thought which is immune from some kind of twisting; therefore it is always fallacious to fix upon some particular form of thought and say, "Ah, that consists purely of ideology and rationalization." Let us be quite frank about it. If it is true that the products of thinking in the realms of natural theology can be and sometimes are idolatrous, the same thing is true in the sphere of revelational theology. That too can culminate in some form of

[1] Arthur Koestler, *The Age of Longing* (New York: Macmillan, 1951), p. 83. Used by permission of the publisher.

idolatry. The living God of the Bible is not necessarily identical with the God excogitated by the Biblical theologian.

We are all subject to this danger. All our thinking is infected by a desire not only to attain the truth, but at the same time to affirm social and personal values which, because we are what we are and where we are, we want to affirm. This process is always fundamentally idolatrous, a way of pretending to ourselves and to others that God wishes what we wish, that He confirms and is the source of our prejudices and preferences. But the burden is not to be borne by natural theology alone, or by metaphysics and philosophy alone. Wherever men are men, and wherever sinful men are thinking and seeking the truth, they have to arm themselves and guard themselves against such temptations as these.

Thus, it is always necessary for us to scrutinize and cross-examine our intellectual consciences in order to detect within ourselves, before it is too late, any tendency to make an ideological use of our religious and theological beliefs. There exists a group of Christians in the United States who are banded together for the propagation of the belief (they even publish a small journal devoted to this theme) that what is called a "free economy" has a special divine sanction that raises it above all other economic systems and that it exists where it does exist, and must be brought into existence where it does not exist, in accordance with the will of God.

I once heard a distinguished professor of economics at Geneva, a member of the Swiss Reformed Church, expound precisely the same view. The capitalist free economy was for him the Christian economy.

Perhaps an even more widespread example of the same kind of error is the prevalent tendency to suppose that there is something especially Christian about the democratic way of organizing our political life. I am not thinking here of the way in which many non-Christian thinkers tend to turn democracy into a kind of religion in its own right, with much talk of democratic values, the democratic way of life, and even the democratic virtues, and so on. What I have in mind is a tendency on the part of many Christians to speak of democracy almost as though it were part of their faith.

Now I have no doubt that in appropriate circumstances both a free market economy and a democratic polity can be excellent things. Even then, however, as we know too well, both are liable to corruption. As with all other economies and polities, neither can function efficiently except in a society where workers and citizens reverence justice and fair dealing and are imbued with an integrity of purpose and motive, worship God, and strive to practice the Christian virtues.

In the last resort, all economies and polities are constructed by fallen men in a fallen world. All of them are precarious and in danger of judgment. A free economy will not flourish long, or secure justice and human happiness, in a merely selfish wealth-worshipping society. No democratic polity can secure its foundations or prolong its life in a world of individualists who seek only their own preferences and pleasures. In other words, both of these things

59

can be excellent and desirable forms in their own way, but neither of them is a part of the divine dispensation, and neither of them is immune from the judgment of God.

There is no way of winning total immunity, save by the grace of God. The thinker, remember, requires the grace of God just as much as anyone else—not that the thinker is a peculiar kind of man, for no man spends the whole of his life thinking, and presumably few men pass through the whole of their lives without ever thinking. But whenever a man is thinking deliberately and systematically and saying, in effect, "Under the providence of God, some work of thought is my vocation," let him remember that, just as much as any other man whose life is dedicated to any other form of activity, he needs the grace of God not only to save and redeem him but also to sanctify him and keep him on the right pathway for his particular vocation. This is important for us all, whether we attempt to adumbrate some kind of natural theology or not.

CHAPTER THREE

THE ACHIEVEMENT OF NATURAL THEOLOGY

In this chapter we shall have to consider how far, taking both the past and the present into account, the kind of thinking which we call natural theology has produced any results of positive and lasting value. We shall have to treat the subject in very broad outline indeed. Nothing like a history of natural theology will be possible within the restricted space at our disposal. Instead, we shall have to summarize what seems to me the essence of various types of natural theology with very little attempt to give them the individual flavor which they naturally possess in the context of the work and thought of any particular writer. Again, we shall be able to consider natural theology only in what seems to me to be its very best forms. Of course, the history of natural theology is littered with bad arguments, just like the history of any kind of theology—or any kind of anti-theology, for that matter. In other words we shall confine ourselves in most cases to broadly summarized, non-individuated types of thought which possess some kind of permanent and abiding validity or interest.

The Cosmological Argument in Philosophical Dress

The argument from the existence of the world to the existence of God—that is, to the existence of some kind of directive agency which transcends and yet is responsible for, and therefore implied by, the existence of the world—can choose either of two distinct points of departure. It can begin simply with the mere fact that there is a world, however much or however little we may know about it, and argue in a purely philosophical way about the implications of finite and contingent existence. An argument of this kind will be possible and perhaps valid even if we know nothing whatever about the world except the fact of its mere existence. Alternatively, the cosmological argument may select for its point of departure some kind of scientific knowledge which we suppose ourselves to possess about the world, in which case, of course, its validity may be undermined by the subsequent course of scientific speculation and research.

In the case of any particular writer it is often difficult to determine whether his point of departure is scientific or philosophical. Thus, Aristotle probably began with his scientific beliefs about the nature of the physical universe and the processes characteristic of it—his *Metaphysics*, as the name implies, is intended to be a kind of sequel to his *Physics*—but in later centuries his arguments had much more influence on philosophers than on physical scientists, and they gradually detached themselves from their original basis in Greek science. Thus, St. Thomas Aquinas, the great

62

Christian Aristotelian, can point out that it makes no difference to arguments of this kind whether the physical universe had any beginning in time or not. This is St. Thomas's way of detaching the kind of cosmological argument that he inherited from Aristotle from any particular scientific belief about the nature of the physical universe. In his view the mere fact of the existence of the physical universe—a kind of existence, that is, which is finite and contingent and altogether incapable of explaining its own reality—proves the existence of God and will prove the existence of God even if its form and appearance were quite different from that which we know from our experience and our sciences it in fact possesses. This is the purely philosophical version of the argument. Not merely this physical universe but any kind of physical universe whatsoever can prove the existence of God.

This gives us the essence of all forms of the cosmological argument, however clumsy or however profound. Physical existence in its very nature is finite and contingent. It does not have to be as it is, for we can quite easily imagine that it may be otherwise. It does not even have to be at all, for we can quite easily imagine its nonexistence. It simply *happens to be*. It has always an inescapably, accidental character. This is what the philosophers mean when they say that physical existence is contingent. Such an assertion is not a scientific proposition, for it is equally true in any conceivable or imaginable kind of physical universe whatsoever. In other words, the observation that the physical universe, any physical universe, must be contingent is not the kind of proposition which can either be confirmed or refuted by any possible inductive survey or analysis of the facts and processes of which it is made up. Any such reality is a contingent reality which might conceivably, that is without logical self-contradiction, have been otherwise or not have been at all.

All forms of the cosmological argument amount in essence to this: an insistence that contingent being can only exist if there is some necessary being which is responsible for the contingency. Contingent being, being that merely happens to be, can only be explained if we infer from it the existence of necessary being, being that has to be, and being that carries within itself the necessity and ground of its own existence. This is not necessarily an argument for what has been called first cause. Quite conceivably, the physical universe may have existed from all eternity and may have had no beginning in time at all. But even so, it cannot explain its own existence. An eternal physical system will still be a contingent physical system, which might have been otherwise than it is and might even not have been at all.

Another way of expressing substantially the same argument is to dwell on the contrast between actuality and possibility. In this world many more things may possibly happen than those which actually do happen. Because I am here in my study composing these particular sentences, I am not in any one of the many other places in which I might equally well have been. Nobody would have said that the laws of reality had been flouted or outraged if, instead, I had taken the morning off and gone to visit a friend or gone out into the town to do a little personal shopping. Every event seems to select one among many alternatives which

64

would have been equally possible, and in selecting this one possibility to negate all the others. Thus, the passage from mere possibility to concrete actuality seems always to depend upon some kind of selective activity which transcends the event itself. Once we see that the existence of this universe as a whole is similarly a fact which selects one possibility from among innumerable others, it becomes clear that the existence of the universe implies one supreme, transcendent selective activity, apart from which the coming into existence of anything else would have been inconceivable.

Considered simply in itself, then, the sheer givenness, the brute factuality of the universe is not rational. Science as such can take the observed facts of the universe for its point of departure, and defer to the facts with a kind of humble natural piety which, from the Christian point of view, is one of the best, most valid, and ennobling aspects of the scientific attitude. But philosophy cannot take sheer factuality as its point of departure. For philosophy factuality itself lies at the very heart of the mystery. Why any facts? Why these particular facts? The question which philosophy asks cannot be asked in terms of the facts simply because the mystery of the sheer factuality of the facts constitutes the essential question. That is why purely philosophical arguments are quite independent of any particular state of scientific knowledge. They have precisely the same degree of validity in an age of biological evolution and atomic physics as they possessed centuries ago before any of these scientific developments were thought of. The answers to such philosophical questions do not tell us more about the facts, or even help us to relate the facts to one another in a more satisfactory way. They simply help to clear up for us the problem of what is involved in the sheer factuality of the facts, any facts, facts known to us or facts unknown.

The validity of this type of argument is thus quite independent of the existing state of our scientific knowledge. But what measure of validity do arguments of this kind possess? It seems to me obvious that *if* we are justified in trusting our reason to take us this far, to push beyond the stage of scrutinizing and relating facts to one another into the deeper waters in which we seek to ask and answer questions about ultimate being itself, then the argument which concludes "that because contingent being exists necessary being must exist" is one which carries with it, to say the least, a very high degree of probability and conviction.

We must admit, on the other hand, that the particular *if* is a very big *if* indeed. Since the time of Emmanuel Kant a considerable number of philosophers have doubted whether the human reason can be trusted to carry us this far. They have held that the human reason is a finite and pragmatic instrument designed by nature to enable us to cope with the facts of life, but certainly not designed by nature to carry us beyond the facts of life into the sphere of those deeper questions about ultimate reality in the service of which traditional philosophy and natural theology have endeavored to employ it. I have already discussed the kind of critical philosophy which seeks to delimit and restrict the scope of the human reason. I think, myself, that this kind of philosophy is probably mistaken in its aim. I am convinced that to delimit and restrict the scope of human reason by a self-critical rational activity is a mistaken and self-contradictory enterprise. Reason cannot trace its own boundaries without transcending its own boundaries. In other words, the so-called critical philosophy is continually guilty of arguing "in a circle."

Nevertheless, although I *think* that this kind of philosophy is probably mistaken, I am not in a position, nor is anyone else, to say that it is certainly mistaken. For this reason I do not care to claim, with many Roman Catholic philosophers, that the cosmological kind of argument, at its very best, demonstrates the bare existence of God beyond all rational doubt. I prefer to say that it makes the existence of God highly probable, much more probable indeed than any alternative hypothesis.

What this kind of argument really depends upon is a faith in human reason, a belief that sheer reason is capable, when functioning with a maximum degree of analytic power and intellectual integrity—which, of course, in a fallen world it rarely does—of conducting us into the very heart of the profoundest mysteries of ultimate being. The philosophical way of believing in God thus rests upon, and is intimately connected with, a profound faith in the human reason as among the very highest of God's gifts to men. It is perhaps no small thing to have thus perceived and defined the close connection between our faith in God and our faith in reason.

Our faith in God supports our faith in reason because it indicates that reason is no mere animal attribute, which man has slowly evolved and perfected through time as a pragmatic weapon by means of which he may wrestle with and overcome his physical environment. On the contrary, it affirms that reason is one of those characteristic spiritual gifts in virtue of which we are able to say that man is made in the image of God. After all, it would not be sufficient if man were merely a rational being in an irrational universe. That would be as futile a situation as that of a being equipped with the sense of hearing in a universe in which there was nothing to be heard. There is not much point in being rational except in a rational universe. To be equipped by nature always to look out for the rational in a universe in which in fact nothing is rational would be a frustrating and an inefficacious condition. Then, too, we cannot make much sense of what we may call the pragmatic success of reason unless we suppose that there is a reason over against us, a reason eminently in and transcendently behind the things we reason about, as well as a reason within us. But if faith in God, which is, among many other things, a faith in an ultimate and utterly effective reason, thus reinforces and sustains our faith in reason itself, then we shall be more inclined to listen to the kind of reasoning which sustains and gives rational conviction to our faith in God by discovering in Him the clue to the mystery of the existence of everything that is less than God. Faith in God sustains faith in reason, and faith in reason reinforces faith in God. At first sight this looks rather similar to a circular argument, but the "circle" is not in fact an argument at all; it is the circle of completeness, the rounded, satisfying pattern which our arguments assume in relation to one another once we have brought them to something like perfection.

The Cosmological Argument in Scientific Dress

In its purest and probably its best form the cosmological argument, as we have seen, is independent of any particular state of our scientific knowledge, but from time to time attempts have been made to elaborate arguments for the existence of God by showing that He is implied by certain particular scientific theories or basic scientific principles. Such arguments have the disadvantage that they may be rendered out of date by further advances in scientific theory, but so long as the doctrines and principles which they employ remain in vogue they may have a certain limited value and force. Most arguments of this kind are not so much arguments for the existence of God as attempts to show that the world must have had a beginning in time. They are thus arguments for the necessity of believing in a creation. But a creation presumably implies a creator, and such arguments are therefore arguments for the existence of God, at least by implication.

Certainly, if it can be shown that the physical universe had a beginning in time and has only existed for a finite time, such an item of knowledge will go far toward confirming the philosopher's view, if it needs any such confirmation, that the physical universe is contingent. Strictly speaking, it does not require any such confirmation. As we have seen, St. Thomas Aquinas was right to perceive that the existence of the universe would be contingent even if it had no beginning in time. Nevertheless, the fact that the universe had a beginning in time, if it can be scientifically established, will certainly corroborate the belief that its existence is neces-

sarily contingent. If, however, scientific forms of the cosmological argument can do no more than corroborate the philosophical belief in the contingency of the universe, they still
require reinforcement by some form of the philosophical
cosmological argument if they are to push beyond demonstrating that the universe had a beginning in time to the
conclusion that such a beginning in time necessarily points
to the existence of a creator who transcends both time and
the physical universe altogether. In other words, the scientific forms of the cosmological argument do not really replace, or substitute for, the philosophical form; they are
more like attempts to verify in scientific terms the minor
premise of the philosophical argument. The philosophical
argument may be schematised in the traditional syllogistic
form somewhat as follows:

Major premise: contingent being is inexplicable apart from
 necessary being.
Minor premise: The physical universe is a contingent being.
Conclusion: The physical universe is inexplicable apart
 from necessary being.

This brief summary-formula will indicate at once that scientific forms of the cosmological argument can do no more,
at best, than supply us with additional reasons, and we already have very good reasons, apart from the physical sciences, for believing that the minor premise is true. Thus
arguments of this kind cannot do more than make a very
subordinate contribution to the cosmological argument as
a whole.

No doubt, if we view the question from a purely pragmatic point of view the citation of prevalent scientific theories and evidences in support of Christian beliefs does make for effective apologetics. Most of our contemporaries have an almost superstitious reverence for anything that can plausibly be called scientific, and hence they are apt to be impressed by arguments that employ scientific concepts and that appeal to received scientific theories. But the genuine Christian theologian or philosopher is not in the first place interested in effective apologetics. He is not a sophist or paid advocate, chiefly concerned to persuade other people. He is a man with an intellectual conscience chiefly concerned to satisfy his own reason, just as any other scientist or philosopher who works in any other field of study and reflection. I believe that in the long run the Christian thinker will even be more effective as an apologetic force if he puts his primary stress on the virtue of absolute intellectual honesty. The history of Christian thought is littered with defective arguments for Christianity, which have enjoyed, at first, a certain temporary success, but which ended by embarrassing the whole case for Christianity once their defectiveness was generally realized. Real faith disdains the unreliable assistance of bad arguments.

There can be no doubt that many of the arguments for Christianity drawn from passing phases of the development of scientific thought have been very defective. A particularly unfortunate tendency is the habit, characteristic of many Christians who work in the natural sciences, of calling in the assistance of the concept of God to help them out at the point where their existing scientific theories and concepts are inadequate to explain the phenomena. Newton was one of the most celebrated of those who offended in this particular way. The late R. G. Collingwood has an adverse comment on Newton's alleged scientific argument for the existence of God which puts the matter in a nutshell:

He argues, that since we cannot, on his own principles, explain why all the planets revolve in the same direction round the sun, or why their orbits are so disposed that they never bump into one another, this "supremely elegant structure of the solar system cannot have arisen except by the device and power of an intelligent being," thus exalting the limitations of his own method into a proof of the existence of God.[1]

We are all familiar, of course, with the final result of Newton's gross philosophical error. Laplace, a hundred years later, so refined and extended the Newtonian account of the physical universe that he explained the phenomena, which had so baffled Newton, within the terms of the Newtonian theory. Hence, when Napoleon asked him why there was nothing about God in his book, he replied with the famous words, "I have no need of that hypothesis"—as indeed he had not.

The truth is that an argument for the existence of God of the Newtonian type is not really an argument based on the existing state of scientific knowledge at all. Instead, it is an argument based on the existing state of scientific ignorance, an argument almost surely destined to have its foundations undermined by further scientific progress. It is this bad habit of devising arguments for religion on the basis of a temporary stage in the development of scientific knowledge

[1] R. S. Collingwood, *The Idea of Nature* (New York: Oxford), p. 108. Used by permission of the publisher.

which has given rise to the impression that scientific progress, step by step, destroys the arguments that support our religious beliefs. In one sense, this prevalent impression is correct. Scientific progress has removed, and does remove, many of the arguments which Christians have employed in support of their beliefs. But the arguments which it removes are the bad ones. Thus, the process is not really a threat to Christianity at all, but rather a merciful purgation of Christian intellectualism.

Rather more respectable than drawing arguments from passing phases of scientific thought, is the attempt to show that certain basic scientific postulates, as distinct from developed scientific theories, do clearly indicate the contingency of the whole world-process. Thus, the late Prof. A. E. Taylor advanced an argument based on the so-called laws of thermodynamics:

One of the first principles of the science of Thermodynamics is the so-called "principle of Carnot" or "law of the dissipation of energy." In virtue of this principle, heat always tends to pass from a body of higher temperatures to bodies of lower. The hotter body tends to impart heat to colder bodies in its vicinity, so that it becomes cooler and they warmer. It follows that at the end of a period of time which, however long, must be finite the heat of our stellar universe must ultimately be distributed uniformly over its whole extent; change, variety, and life, must thus be lost in one dreary monotony. But if we ask why these dismal consequences have not as yet occurred, we are driven to assume that at a remote, but still finite, distance of past time the distribution of heat through the stellar universe must have been one which, on mathematical principles, is infinitely improbable.[2]

[2] A. E. Taylor, "The Vindication of Religion," *Essays Catholic and Critical* (London: S.P.C.K.), p. 37. Used by permission of the publisher.

The point is that if we take this basic principle seriously, we seem to be compelled to acknowledge that any physical universe in which such a law is operative cannot recede infinitely into past time. In other words, the universe must have had a beginning, must have arisen out of a state of affairs not characterized by this particular principle at all.

More recently not unsimilar arguments have been put forward by people working in the field of atomic physics. Such investigators argue that it is now possible to calculate with some precision how long the processes which in this atomic age we take to be the elemental processes at work in the physical universe have in fact been going on. Thus, we know the rate at which lead is changing into thorium; we also know, with approximate correctness, how much lead and how much thorium there are in the world. Such data enable us to calculate with some precision the period of time that lead has been changing into thorium. If the processes with which atomic physicists are concerned are indeed the processes which constitute the very essence of the life of the physical universe, then indeed, such data would seem to compel us to believe that the physical universe had a definite beginning in time.

The validity of arguments of this kind depends on our attitude toward basic scientific principles, and this is a question concerning which philosophers of science differ very sharply. It is always possible, of course, to receive and contemplate the basic principles and most widely accepted doctrines of the various sciences in what I will call a spirit of naïve realism. Such a spirit regards the basic principles of science as referring to and describing an actually existing state of affairs. This means that we regard the sciences as producers of sheer objective truth, in the simplest and most straightforward sense of the word.

This is precisely how many people, perhaps most people, do in fact regard the sciences. There are, however, grave difficulties about this view. All of the sciences have a history, and in the past many principles and doctrines, now outmoded, have been regarded as objectively true, because they conformed to all the known facts, were fully supported by all available experimentation, and enabled people to predict future events and exercise some kind of technical control over nature. Thus, the pre-Copernican, Ptolemaic astronomer believed that the earth was in the center of the physical universe and that the sun and the planets moved around it. This, of course, is now an utterly rejected theory, yet the pre-Copernican was able in his own day to predict eclipses of the sun and the moon, to forecast movements of the planets, and to interpret in terms of his theory all the known facts that were felt to be relevant.

More recently, we have had other great changes in our basic scientific attitudes, for example the transition from Newtonian to relativity physics, and doubtless we shall have many more in the future.

These considerations make it difficult for us to receive prevalent scientific doctrines and postulates in anything like a mood of simple faith. Considerations of this kind have led many philosophically inclined scientists and many philosophers interested in the analysis and interpretation of science (these are two distinct groups, although they have much in common) to hold that scientific doctrines and principles are no more than convenient and pragmatic axioms which enable us to handle and control our physical environment in practice. If we hold this view, we must indeed base our practice on the doctrines of science, but we must never assert them or reason from them as though they were absolute or objective truth.

Now is not the place to enter into this question in any detail, nor have I the requisite time and space at my disposal. In its own way the pragmatic view raises as many difficulties as the naïvely realistic one, for, we may well ask, how can scientific doctrines or principles have the immense pragmatic effectiveness of, for example, contemporary atomic physics, if they are entirely unrelated to absolute objective truth? It seems obvious that we are not warranted to suppose that scientific doctrines and basic principles constitute the whole truth about the physical universe. But is it really possible for us to suppose, in total reaction against the realistic view, that they are no more than convenient fictions? The truth must surely lie somewhere between these two extreme interpretations of science. The upshot of this present discussion for us, however, is clear. The type of argument we have been discussing only holds good if we assume the validity of a certain way of interpreting scientific theories. These arguments *appear* to be based on scientific data and conclusions, but in fact they are based on a philosophy of science which today is widely called in question and is, to that extent at least, open to grave doubt.

To many readers this implication that the meaning of science for us depends, not merely upon what the sciences themselves have to tell us, but also upon what particular philosophy of science we adopt, will appear a strange and disconcerting one. Yet, such is in fact the case. Just as in a democracy the legislature frames and passes the laws, and then leaves it to the judges in the courts to decide precisely what they mean, so, in the last resort, the interpretation of the meaning of scientific theories is the function not of the scientists themselves but of the philosophers of science, or of the scientists themselves in so far as they are also philosophers of science.

A distinguished contemporary scholar, who has given special attention to the way in which modern science grew out of the Christian philosophy of the middle ages, Mr. A. C. Crombie, stresses the gulf that divides science from metaphysics:

Scientific theory then, tells us no more than it appears to tell us about the experimental facts, namely that they may be related in a particular manner. It can provide no grounds for the belief that the entities postulated for the purposes of the theory actually exist. So, whether or not science makes metaphysical assumptions, as scientific theory it has no metaphysical implications. It can never be used either to support or contradict interpretations of experience written in another language or in a different mood, and propositions in other languages and moods have nothing to do with science. Dives was separated from Lazarus no farther than science is from theology or ethics or a theory of beauty. To try to pass from one to the other is to land in the chaos between.[3]

Perhaps the closing sentences exaggerate a little. The gulf between science and philosophy can indeed be bridged,

[3] A. C. Crombie, *Grosseteste and Experimental Science* (New York: Oxford), p. 319. Used by permission of the publisher.

77

and has in fact been bridged, in various ways. But the gulf can only be bridged from the philosophical side, and the supports upon which the bridge rests are of philosophical not scientific manufacture.

Still another kind of argument, which has at least a highly scientific flavor, takes for its point of departure some of the analogies and illustrations frequently employed by scientific thinkers in communicating and imaginatively interpreting the achievements of science to that large public which is enthralled and fascinated by science but is not equipped to understand its language. Thus, for example, there was a lengthy period during which many scientific workers were particularly interested in the construction of working mechanical models of physical processes (as they conceived them).

This was the age of "mechanistic science," an age that delighted to liken reality to a vast machine. Of course, this likening of physical reality to a machine was never really anything more than an illustrative analogy, but there is no doubt that many philosophers and scientists took the analogy very seriously. Analogies of this kind are often very useful, but they should always be employed for illustrative and communicative purposes and never asserted as literal objective truth.

And an analogy does not need to be true. Indeed, in the nature of the case it cannot be true. We rightly require of an analogy no more than that it should be illuminating, and some analogies are indeed much more illuminating than others. It is always dangerous in any sphere of thought to take our analogies too seriously, and it is impossible, in any sphere of thought, to avoid employing some analogy or other.

It has, however, been pointed out by some philosophers, —the late Prof. J. E. Turner, for example—that if we do treat the mechanistic analogy seriously enough, it points in a theistic direction. All the real machines with which we are acquainted have been constructed by intelligent beings to serve their own conscious purposes. If the physical universe really is a machine, then it certainly indicates the existence of a supreme intelligent and purposive being who has devised it to serve his own supremely intelligent ends.

This was, of course, no new idea of Prof. Turner's. In the eighteenth century the deistic philosophers and orthodox Christian apologists (*e.g.* the once celebrated Archdeacon Paley) were particularly fond of likening the physical universe to some mechanical contrivance, such as a watch, and then arguing that such a universe necessarily implied the existence of God just as the watch implied the existence of the watchmaker. Often this analogical argument was given a deistic twist. God had created the perfect machine which, once created, operated forever without requiring any further attention from the celestial engineer. But the deistic interpretation rather spoiled the analogy. We know of no machines which once created require no further attention. On the contrary, machines as we know them must be continually serviced and fed. We feed coal and water to our steam engines; we lubricate and refuel our automobiles. Our machines require our constant attention, not merely because they are imperfect and often operate badly, but because it is part of their essential nature to require our attention, so

79

that only if they are given special care can they operate in accordance with the intentions of their designers. No, if we are to take the mechanistic analogy seriously it requires, not merely the remote, indifferent God of the deists, who creates but does not provide, but the infinitely concerned, responsibility bearing God of the Bible, to whom must be attributed not only the act of creation but also the infinite activities of providence.

The mechanistic argument is a simple and attractive one, and it has a certain force for men who are in the habit of trying to bring the abstract theories of mathematical science to life by imaginatively likening them to the machines with which we are so familiar in our everyday experience. The defect of the argument is, however, obvious. It takes the analogy far too seriously. As we can all see, the physical universe is not in fact a machine, and does not even resemble one to any significant extent. No doubt it is illuminating in certain contexts and for certain purposes to liken the physical universe to a machine, but that is a very different thing from roundly asserting that it *is* a machine. The mechanistic interpretation of science is neither science nor philosophy. It is poetry, and as in all poetry the images which convey the meaning do not have to be asserted or believed in, in order to be meaningful. To say that the physical universe or some portion of it is really like a vast machine is a statement of the same kind as that which the poet makes when he declares that his "love is like a red, red rose." In both cases we can appreciate the force and meaning of the comparison, and we can be deeply impressed by it, but we are not required to believe it or assert it in any literal sense.

The main conclusion of this section of our discussion is clearly a negative one. The attempt to give the cosmological type of argument for the existence of God a scientific flavor is not particularly successful, and it can yield no result of any special importance. At best, efforts of this kind can do little more than corroborate from another point of view some of the conclusions which many of the classical philosophers had reached independently of any scientific considerations. If the cosmological argument pretends that it is a purely scientific argument, it only succeeds in being pseudo-scientific. Nowadays many people are irrationally impressed by a citation of the authority of science. But no honest natural theology can stoop to exploiting this gullibility. Natural theology is a candid and sincere endeavor to appeal to the rational in man. It is not a formula for impressing the irrational. The popular deference to the authority of a science, whose strength, real achievements, and ultimate limitations alike the populace is quite incapable of understanding, is the supreme superstition of our age.

The Existential Argument: Personal Form

As I remarked in an earlier chapter, the existential approach to the problems of religion and the existence of God is not really as distinct from and independent of the cosmological approach as its supporters often suppose. This type of approach discovers and experiences the contingency of the real in the realm of self-conscious human existence rather than in that of the physical universe, and its argument from contingent to necessary being is often so expressed as to be almost indistinguishable from the claim that self-conscious contingent being, whenever it is aware of itself with sufficient profundity, experiences the reality of the necessary being as something inextricably bound up with its own existence. In other words, this type of approach is apt to claim that the existence of God is experienced rather than merely inferred.

This is an antithesis which must not be pressed too far. There is a sense in which it is true that all conscious experience is a very simple form of inference, and certainly it is often true that we may validly infer anything that we consciously experience. I may say that I do not have to infer the existence of the table in front of me because I experience its existence. Some philosophers will reply, however, that to experience its existence is really to infer its existence from the fragmentary sense data which constitute my primary experience. Even if we do not go as far as this and allow for some real distinction between inference and experience, it can only be on the basis that experience is in some way a more profound and more embracing concept than inference. Inference is part of experience; whatever is validly experienced can also be inferred.

We must not distinguish too much between those who claim to infer the existence of God, as something which they find logically *implied* by finite and contingent existence, and those who claim to experience the existence of God as a reality *implicit* in finite and contingent existence. No doubt there is a distinction. If I say that x implies y, I mean that the reality of x is a kind of signpost which points towards the reality of y, a reality y which is both bound up with and external to its own reality. If I say, however, that the reality of y is implicit in the reality of x, I mean that a profounder consciousness of the reality of x will of itself bring the reality of y within the orbit of my experience. In other words, that I am not fully conscious of the reality of x until I have become co-conscious of the reality of both x and y. In so far, therefore, as I understand the Christian doctrine of the relation between God and His creatures, it affirms both these things: the imminent reality of God is implicit in the reality of His creatures, and at the same time the reality of His creatures implies the transcendent reality of God. Thus, both approaches are valid and important, and the distinction between them must not be overstressed.

When we turn to the leading existentialist philosophers themselves, however, we find them profoundly disagreeing about whether the reality of God is found implicit in human existence, if we explore its meaning in sufficient depth and profundity. They may be roughly divided into the religious existentialists, for whom, in the words of Kierkegaard, "it is the God-relationship that makes a man a man," and the irreligious existentialists who, although vividly aware of the limitations, the finiteness, and contingency of man (for them supremely summed up and experienced in the ultimate fact of his mortality), tend to conceive of man as ultimately alone with his inescapable fate. They may, like Nietzsche, dream of some way in which man may ultimately overcome the limitations inherent in his finitude and become God, or they may alternatively, like John Paul Sartre and some of the contemporary French existentialists, think of man as heroically and stoically enduring his fate, and even defying it with his freedom, until at last and inevitably it comes upon him and strikes him down. About what we have called the contingency of man, however, even though they would probably prefer not to use the word, they are all completely agreed. Human existence, as they know it, does not carry its own ground or necessity within it and is inherently frail, finite, and mortal. It can guarantee neither its own continuance nor its own fulfilment.

What divides these two currents of existentialist opinion is not any disagreement about the facts but a disagreement about their interpretation. For the religious existentialists, human destiny and the latent promise of human nature are in fact fulfilled in man's conscious relationship of faith and trust toward God. For the irreligious existentialists, they are never really fulfilled at all. Some bold and hardy spirits, by a supreme and reckless exertion of their freedom, merely come closer to self-fulfilment than others.

As between these two, I cannot doubt that the religious existentialists achieve a more rational interpretation of human existence than the irreligious existentialists. The preoccupation of existentialist philosophy with self-conscious existence, as the most important and revealing element in our experience, is inexplicable and untenable unless we hold that self-conscious spiritual existence is also and ultimately the most important reality in the whole universe. In other words, if human existence is a mere accident in a universe which is blind and indifferent to it, the existentialist preoccupation with human existence is not rationally tenable. The religious existentialists, with their doctrine of the fulfilment of finite selfhood in an existential, personal relationship to the infinite selfhood of God provides us with a scheme which is, from the philosophical point of view, far more satisfactory and convincing. We may say that whereas human existence, for the irreligious existentialist, is in the last resort an irrational and inexplicable tragedy; for the religious existentialist, however tragic many of its component episodes, it is in the last resort a rational, purposeful, and intelligible comedy.

In tragedy terrible events occur, we know not why, and ultimately in vain. In comedy terrible events may occur also, but the conclusion shows us why and shows us that that they are not in vain. Comedy, properly speaking, must be distinguished from mere farce, as Dante clearly saw when he called his epic description of the whole Christian scheme of destiny *The Divine Comedy.* Tragedy is completely locked up in time and therefore ultimately irrational. Comedy is eschatological and rational, always concerned to show how the end makes sense of all that has come before. We may illustrate by comparing Shakespeare's *Hamlet* with his *A Winter's Tale.* The last act of the written tragedy of *Hamlet* is simply the opening of the unwritten tragedy of young Fortinbras, one finite, temporal episode merely leading to another. *A Winter's Tale* on the other hand concludes with an allegory of resurrection and redemption which makes sense of all that has gone before and shows how all things can be transmuted and made new.

The difficulty with comedy, and this is why so many of the greatest tragedies are often finer as literary composi-

tions or even as spiritual documents than the great come-
dies, is that comedy is usually compelled to express its
eschatology in temporal allegories. Comedy, like tragedy,
is compelled to end in time, but, of course, there is no end-
ing in time. Hence, the closing scene of a comedy is always
allegorical: "And they lived happily ever after." Comedy,
thus, cannot be secularized as successfully as can tragedy.
Its essential nature is religious and Biblical, and if it does
not conclude with straight, candidly confessed eschatology;
its only alternative is to resort to lame and unconvincing allegory. Hence, the irreligious existentialists, who are tragic
philosophers, often seem to us more candid and convincing
than the religious existentialists, who are essentially comic
philosophers. At bottom, however, the comic philosophers
are the more rational. They have a sense of intelligible purpose informing all things. They have a sense of ultimate
achievement crowning all things. They sense that existence
has an objective meaning of its own and is not a meaningless something which can only have meaning roughly thrust
upon it by crudely extemporizing as they go along.

There we have it. Either existence has an inherent and
objective meaning of its own or it has none. Either existence
is rational or it is not. If existence has no meaning of its
own, we are powerless to give it any by foisting upon it
some kind of subjective interpretation. The religious existentialists misunderstand the essential spirit and character of
their thought if they allow themselves to have dealings with
any kind of irrationalism. Make no mistake about it, existentialism, whatever the existentialists may say, is a rationalism, and a very profound one. It is an insistence on being

ultimately rational about the meaning and purpose of human existence; not merely instrumentally rational about the means which we employ in pursuit of our ends.

At first sight this is a somewhat surprising statement. From Kierkegaard onward most existentialists have believed themselves to be in revolt against the arrogance of rationalism, and most nonexistentialist philosophers would agree in interpreting existentialism as an antirational philosophy, and perhaps dismiss it with contempt on that very account. But the antirational passion and prejudice, which we so often find in the writings of the existentialist philosophers, is not really essential to the true genius of existentialism. The essence of existentialism is to insist that our own intimate experience of existence in the world (our experience of the reality of our freedom and of the way in which life again and again frustrates our freedom, our experience of hope and fear and unquenchable spiritual need, our experience of life and its inescapable fragility and impermanence as it confronts the necessity of death, our experience of love and its disappointment and disillusions) is the most vivid kind of experience of reality which we enjoy and that it constitutes the proper and necessary point of departure in philosophy.

The rationalism against which existentialism properly and necessarily protests is a high and dry rationalism which sins against its own ideal by ignoring and abstracting from our experience of existence. This is the dead rationalism which reasons about everything except the concrete existence which is the most real thing that we know. It is the abstract rationalism which Kierkegaard detected, perhaps not quite accurately, in the great Hegel and denounced, perhaps not quite justly, with such unsparing vehemence. This is also the scientific empiricism which is empirical about everything except about our own existence and which patiently studies and humbly defers to every experience except the most vivid experience of all.

The true existentialist has his own kind of rationalism which sees in the life of reason, motivated and sustained by the rational man's profound existential need for the truth at all costs, and taking the whole range of human experience for its parish, one of the very highest forms of human existence. Let our reasoning but insist upon being a concrete reasoning about the central themes of human existence, rather than an abstract reasoning about isolated problems which a sophisticated reasoning has itself defined and created, and we shall see at once that some kind of existentialist philosophy becomes a rational necessity. John Paul Sartre once wrote a little book dedicated to the proposition that "Existentialism is a humanism." This seems to me a proposition too obviously true to require enforcing. I would only add that, properly understood, existentialism is a rationalism also.

Once again the analogy and parallelism between the cosmological and existential kind of natural theology are clearly brought out. Both of them emphasize the kinship between faith in God and faith in reason. The existentialist preoccupation with existence, as the fundamental and indispensable point of departure in philosophy, is not rational and must in the last resort be abandoned unless we can also hold that existence, the kind of reality with which we are so vividly confronted in the intimacies and depths of our self-knowledge, is objectively speaking the most fundamental and primary form of reality. Self-conscious existence can only be our proper point of departure in philosophy if we can at the same time hold that self-conscious existence is the ultimate and primary form of objective reality itself. Thus again, we are led to the view that there is an essential connection between faith in God and faith in reason.

Faith in reason implies more than that reason is the best instrument we possess for doing what we want to do. Faith in reason means that the universe, and the existence within the universe of such beings as we know and discover ourselves to be, is a rational state of affairs, the meaning and purpose of which can only be disclosed to self-conscious rational beings, and the meaning and purpose of which can only be achieved and exemplified in the existence of self-conscious rational beings. Thus, the existence of self-conscious rational beings is the clue to the meaning of the universe. And this can only be true if self-conscious rational existence is the supreme and absolute fact that underlies and sustains all the existence that there is. Once more, then, faith in God sustains faith in reason. And such a faith in reason as I have endeavored to describe ultimately reinforces faith in God.

The Existential Argument: Social Form

We turn our attention now from the subtle intimacies and privacies of self-conscious personal existence to what we may call the social dimensions of personality. Personal existence is not in fact a solitary thing, however solitary some existentialist philosophers make it appear to be. All personal existence is existence in society. It is not of the essence of personality to be solitary. Where this happens it is a tragic accident. There may indeed be deep levels of personal life which we cannot share with our fellows, not even with our most intimate friends, but these are morbid and unhealthy levels unless we can learn in prayer and worship to share them with God. True personal existence is thus essentially and inescapably bound up with other existing persons. It is existence in inescapable communication with *the other*. Indeed only in society can individuals develop into persons, and only in society can they continue to be persons.

Nevertheless many thinkers have labored to establish a kind of antithesis between society, with its rules, regulations, and insistence that members discipline themselves to meet its basic requirements, and individual personality with its demand for freedom and self-expression. In the world, and in life as we know it, such an antithesis often is plausible enough. There is often a real clash between personality and society, but this is a consequence of the corruption of both personality and society in a fallen world. It is not a conflict demanded and brought about by the essential natures of personality and society. Such a conflict is a consequence, as Christians say, of the Fall.

The Fall has brought about a radically unnatural state of human affairs. It has brought about a state of affairs in which personality cannot do without society but, because society as we know it is corrupt, personality cannot be entirely happy and contented within it. Similarly, it has brought it about that society cannot exist and flourish without personality but, because personality is everywhere corrupt, society is constantly tempted to saddle it with a heavy burden of constraint and excessive authority. Hence it happens that human history is characterized by a pendulum-like swing between a state of affairs in which personality enjoys more liberty than corrupt personality can safely be trusted to use wisely and well, and another equally extreme state of affairs in which society is vested with more authority than corrupt society is able to exercise justly and tolerantly.

Properly understood, however, the social is one necessary dimension of personal existence, and we can no more escape from society than we can evade the responsibilities of personality itself. This is an obvious fact which no sanely balanced, truly empirical existentialism can afford to ignore. Existentialism is not individualism, and it mistakes its own nature if it thinks that it is.

The question now before us is this: Can we discern in social life a basic finitude or contingency, a deep seated need for religion and a religious attitude which will enable us to say that an ultimate religious orientation is indispensable to harmonious and fruitful social existence? This is a question with which several important contemporary writers have profoundly concerned themselves. We may mention in particular the writings of Christopher Dawson and many of the basic teachings contained in Arnold Toynbee's A Study of History. The former lays great stress on the universality of religion and of the religious origins of almost all the great forms and vehicles of civilized existence. Toynbee attempts

91

to show that the great crises in and through which a people advance to civilization, and maintain itself there, are in the last analysis crises which have an inescapably religious character and call for description in religious language.

Mr. Dawson's insistence on the universality of religion and the necessary role of religion in the creation and preservation of culture is perhaps most clearly set forth and summarized in his book *Religion and Culture*. Here he stresses the religious origins of the state, the politically organized and unified social order, the concepts of law, science, art, and the idealisms which motivate social criticism and social progress. He maintains this point of view on the basis of a wide range of anthropological and sociological data, and then, in a subsequent volume, *Religion and the Rise of Western Culture*, concentrates on displaying and analyzing the essential relationship between Christianity and our own particular Western form of civilization. Of course the facts which he summarizes have been noted by many other contemporary writers. Thus, Bertand de Jouvenel in his important book *Power* stresses the religious origins of the state, a fact which had also impressed Sir James Fraser earlier in this century. Mr. A. C. Crombie, also, in two important and profoundly learned studies, has illustrated the way in which modern Western natural science arose out of Christian philosophical and theological thought and speculation, fertilized and stimulated by its contacts with Arab philosophy during the Middle Ages.

It would certainly appear that there can be little doubt or argument about the facts themselves. It seems overwhelmingly probable that without religion man would never have attained a civilized existence at all, and that without the Christian religion we should certainly not have attained the particular form of civilization which we now possess. The further contention that without religion civilization cannot continue and, in particular, that without Christianity our civilization cannot continue, is, of course, an inference from these facts of more doubtful character. There is clearly a great difference between observing that without religion a civilization would never have come into existence and arguing that without religion civilization cannot continue in existence. It seems at least possible to hold that, although religion was necessary to the birth and maturing of civilization, it is nevertheless not necessary to its further development, and may even be an obstacle to the attainment of its final perfection. To me, of course, this is very improbable, but it is not an altogether impossible point of view.

Certainly, the way in which periods of religious scepticism and widespread alienation from religious practice coincide with periods of social instability, of a loss of nerve on the part of society as it confronts the intimidating ordeals of history, a decline in its belief in its own civilizing mission and will to survive, does seem to suggest that there is a very close and abiding connection between the maintenance of our religious beliefs and institutions and the preservation and progress of our social order. Nevertheless, it must be admitted that the generalizations which such a writer as Mr. Dawson deduces from his facts have not quite the same authority and certainty as his description of the facts themselves.

There are even profoundly religious reasons for dissatisfaction with a kind of argument which seems to suggest that religion should be accepted and practiced for the sake of social survival. It is not the primary function of religion to preserve civilization. It is possible that a religion, widely and sincerely practiced, may tend toward the preservation of the social order, but such a consequence can only be a kind of by-product. Any living religion has profounder purposes and intentions than that.

On the other hand we should remember the inherent limitations of the kind of argument we are considering. It does not even purport to be an argument for Christianity or any other particular religion. Its aims are more modest. It merely attempts to show that religion of some kind is a natural human necessity, necessary to the well-being of men in society. Clearly the affirmation of belief in any particular religion takes us infinitely further, but that is no reason for despising the value of this kind of argument on its own level and within its own limits.

Far profounder is the analysis of the basic factors operative in the birth and growth of civilization which we find in Arnold Toynbee. The terminology in which he defines these basic factors has a religious character which is not accidental but is necessitated by the essential character of the factors themselves. Thus, according to him, civilizations are born and pass through their initial phases of growth in a crisis of "challenge and response." A people are challenged by a set of intimidating circumstances, and their triumphant response to the challenge lays the foundation of their civilized existence. The language is very similar to that in which a modern Christian theologian would describe the process of Biblical revelation. The revelation itself is hidden in a series of 'crisis-events' to which men respond with prophetic understanding and self-committing faith. Our religion is born in a crisis which elicits the response that lays the foundation of both church and creed, and it prolongs itself and deepens its understanding of the position to which it is committed through a series of similar crises. The parallelism and kinship between the two concepts is very plain. The process out of which civilization is born is at least quasi-religious in character.

Again, Toynbee stresses the role of a creative minority in the growth and extension of a civilization. The lives of the members of this creative minority are characterized by a certain rhythm of "withdrawal and return," of which the clearest examples are to be found in the careers of such great religious leaders as Buddha, St. Paul, and Mahomet. There is an apparent withdrawal from society into closer intercourse with the values and realities which are subsequently taken back into society.

We can observe the same rhythm in the history of modern natural science. The applied science which serves social needs and purpose is subsequent, both in logic and in time, to the pure science into which the great scientific discoverers withdraw, and in so doing withdraw from society. But the process itself is at least quasi-religious in character.

Another of Toynbee's key concepts is what he calls "etherealisation." A society may become so successful in its response to the challenge of intimidating circumstances that the circumstances cease to challenge it sufficiently to stimulate it to further creative efforts. What is demanded in these circumstances is a transposition of the challenge to a more inward and spiritual plane, so that the society which no longer finds itself challenged by its physical situation, or the hostility of other societies, may continue to challenge itself from within. Surely, this challenging of itself from within is very close to the concept of a prophetic religion. The prophets challenge their society from within, denouncing its failures and abuses, not because they are hostile to it, but precisely because they love it. It is their labor and their witness which stimulate it to further creative development.

If, according to Toynbee, the processes in and through which civilizations are born and grow are fundamentally of a religious character, it is equally true that for him the disintegration of a civilization has a profoundly irreligious character. Toynbee describes the disintegration of civilization partly in terms of inertia, of a "resting upon one's oars," a failure on the part of the mature civilization to challenge itself any further from within, and partly in terms of what he calls idolatory—a state of mind in which a society comes to give absolute value to its own being and its own achievements. A disintegrating society is a society that worships itself. The theology of such a worship may be some kind of fanatical nationalism, or a humanism which persuades men to concentrate so entirely upon the values which they know, upon the values which illuminate their own contemporary existence, that they can perceive no other values as transcending them. The values upon which the humanist concentrates may be, and probably are, values indeed, but our values, however valuable, will ruin us if we permit them to blind us to all that lies beyond and above them. Thus, for Toynbee, civilization and its growth is the product of a creative spirituality, whereas its disintegration and decline is the consequence of an exhausted spirituality, in which men make idols of themselves and their own achievements.

We may most helpfully contrast and relate Dawson's and Toynbee's approaches to our problem by saying that whereas Dawson indicates the reality of the connection between religion and civilization by building up a vast store of empirical evidence, Toynbee analyzes and interprets the connection by showing that the processes which create and sustain civilization have an ineradicably religious character. What both of them agree in asserting, to fall back upon language which we have employed throughout this chapter, is the contingency of the secular. The secular, the merely temporal and this-worldly, aspects of civilization do not add up to an independent, self-contained whole. We may agree that civilization sometimes appears to be secular in both its spirit and intention, but this is only because we so often ignore the way in which any civilization is rooted in a view of life and the world which is essentially religious. The "world" in the New Testament sense, the merely secular (which the Bible so often contrasts sharply with the Kingdom of God and the Church), is thus an abstract and unreal thing, a tragic illusion. It is society abstracting itself from the realities upon which it depends. Thus it is reduced to worshipping itself, because it recognizes no reality above itself which can and will judge and redeem it.

Wherever we look—outwardly at the physical universe which provides us with our native environment, around us

97

at the life of the society to which we belong, or within us at the intimacies and depths of our own personal existence —we are impressed by the inescapable fact of contingency. Nowhere do we find completeness; nowhere do we find a kind of being which can conceivably either give birth to itself or sustain itself; nowhere do we find anything which carries within itself the ground and explanation of its own existence. The social form of the existential argument points toward the same conclusion as the other types of natural theology which we have so briefly characterized.

The Final Assessment

This ultimate convergence of view, this almost precise parallelism between the types of argument which we have so rapidly surveyed, is in many respects the most impressive thing about them. Probably no one of the arguments which we have considered will by itself produce any high degree of confidence or conviction, but when we set these several considerations side by side and note the unanimity with which, when we analyze what they say, they agree in proclaiming the same fundamental message, our rational nature can hardly fail to be impressed. After all, it is not as though there were any considerable reason on the other side for not believing in God. A theistic philosophy is not logically self-contradictory, nor in any other way repugnant to our reason.

I do not believe that any philosopher can possibly hold that it is impossible for the theistic account of life and the universe to be true. There are, in fact, almost no arguments against the existence of God. There are certainly many difficulties, for example the so-called problem of evil, but then there will certainly be some difficulties in our ultimate philosophy whatever it may be.

In the nature of the case, a philosophical view can do no more than barely outline the form of reality in which it believes. In the realm of philosophy, as we have already seen, we are compelled by the nature of philosophy to infer the reality which our philosophy asserts and to turn the reality into a concept, whereas the reality, whatever else it may be, is certainly not a concept. In the realm of philosophy we are never confronted with that which our philosophy asserts in all its concrete reality. That is why no philosophy, however profoundly and confidently theistic, can ever be a substitute for religion, or of itself prompt and sustain a religion. Of course, the philosophizing of religious men will be religiously motivated, but the religiously minded philosopher, most of all, will always be conscious of the fundamental distinction between religion and philosophy.

To return to the main point, it is certainly not a logical impossibility that the theistic philosophy should be the true one, and it is significant that there are no worthwhile arguments against the existence of God. Atheistic propaganda usually confines itself to criticizing arguments which have been put forward for the existence of God, and it must be admitted that some of these criticisms are often just, because many of the arguments which purport to prove the existence of God have been exceedingly bad ones. Nevertheless, they are not all bad, and I believe we are justified in claiming that taken together they indicate that it is extremely probable that the theistic philosophy is the one which is, at least, most significantly gravitating in the direction of the truth.

I do not think we can hold that theistic philosophy demonstrates the existence of God beyond all possibility of rational doubt (for reasons which I have already indicated), but I think it no exaggeration to suggest that the convergent arguments for theism, and what we may call in the widest sense a religious attitude toward life, are so strong and establish so high a degree of probability that we may assume their substantial truth.

Of course, this is not enough for the Christian. He will say that he has other, more profound and more empirical ways of confirming the truth of the theistic hypothesis. For him, God has not merely been validly inferred by philosophers, but God has actually spoken to men and revealed himself both in Jesus Christ and in the life and experience of the Church. To live and think and worship and pray within the context of the Christian revelation and the Christian Church is to discover that within oneself there is a sharpening of the cool philosophical assessment of probabilities into the basic, rocklike convictions upon which one's whole existence is founded.

Of course, the Christian is fully justified in reporting this experience, and in regarding it as supremely significant. But this experience gives the Christian no ground for depreciating the testimony of philosophy, nor does his personal witness to what God has done for him in Jesus Christ in any way replace or supplant the testimony of philosophy. The philosophical testimony remains valid and illuminating within its own limits.

100

We must always remember that no philosophical argument for a theistic and religious view of life in the world is an argument for becoming a Christian. The arguments for becoming a Christian do not arise in our minds until we begin to make an honest survey of what we may call the Christian facts. By the Christian facts I refer to such things as the acts of God in Jesus Christ and our experience (intellectual, moral, spiritual, social) of life in the Church. It is the analysis and interpretation of these facts which provide us with our reasons for becoming and remaining Christians.

These reasons are good ones. There is nothing irrational about becoming and remaining a Christian. I am convinced that the man who talks loosely and vaguely about "relying on faith rather than on reason" does not know what the words faith and reason really mean. Surely, it is clear that there can not conceivably be any reason for becoming a Christian prior to some kind of analysis and interpretation of the Christian facts. But in this life, the most normal role of reason is to analyze and interpret the facts with which we find ourselves confronted and to suggest appropriate action in regard to them. But although our reasons for becoming and remaining Christians are based on an examination and interpretation of the unique Christian facts, we may nevertheless welcome arguments which seem to suggest, if they are valid and always provided that we are rationally convinced of their validity, that even a chain of reasoning which takes as its point of departure all the facts known to us *except* the Christian facts tells as far as it goes in the same direction.

The kind of philosophizing which we call natural theology can thus contribute no more to Christian theology than a certain limited amount of corroboratory detail, "a touch of verisimilitude to what is in itself a by no means bald and unconvincing narrative" (to borrow, with appreciation, the phraseology of W. S. Gilbert). But even this is no small thing. Natural theology proclaims that because the world, even this fallen world, is God's world, the experience of life within it points mutely and short-sightedly toward the reality which the gospel reveals. If the God who reveals himself to us in the gospels is indeed the creator of the world, this is perhaps no more than we should have expected.

CHAPTER FOUR

NATURAL THEOLOGY IN A NEGATIVE MOOD

So much then for what we may fairly call the positive achievement of natural theology. A rational analysis and interpretation of the facts which confront us in our experience of life and the world, even if we ignore for the moment the specifically Christian and religious types of fact, does seem to point in the theistic direction. At all events we are warranted in saying that if reason is to be trusted at all in such matters the theistic hypothesis is at least a very likely one. The question before us in the present chapter is this: Can natural theology continue the argument a little further and plausibly attempt to show that all known alternative hypotheses are by comparison improbable or even impossible?

If such a negative argument can be made out and sustained it would clearly and enormously strengthen the many stranded positive arguments which we endeavored to summarize in the last chapter. Personally, I think that such an argument can be elaborated in a rationally effective manner.

Not only is theism rationally speaking a probable hypothesis, but the various alternatives which have from time to time occurred to the human mind are, and can be shown to be, by comparison, very improbable indeed. We will now consider briefly what the best known and most important of these alternatives are. Some of them we have discussed already; others have not as yet engaged our attention.

Scepticism, Agnosticism, and Positivism

Very few philosophers indeed have endeavored to maintain a total and dogmatic scepticism about everything. Clearly, a comprehensive scepticism of this kind would necessitate being sceptical even about scepticism, and thus finally indicate the possibility of a way out of scepticism altogether. One is reminded of the advice of the sceptical father to his son. "My boy, always be doubtful about everything. Only a fool is ever certain of anything." "Are you quite sure that's true, father?" replies the son. "Yes, my boy, I'm absolutely certain of it."

The prevalent impression that the natural mood of philosophy is a sceptical one is perhaps due to a misinterpretation of the method of systematic doubt employed by many philosophers in the course of their philosophical arguments. The method of systematic doubt is in fact a dialectical device employed in order to discover what there is in our experience, if there is anything, which cannot possibly be doubted or, alternatively, to diagnose and define the doubts which reason must seek to banish from our minds before we are justified in feeling certain, or relatively certain, about anything. Thus the great French philosopher, Descartes,

attempted to doubt everything, but finally came to the conclusion that there are three things which cannot in fact be
doubted: the personal existence of the man who is doing
the doubting, the lucid truths of pure mathematics, and the
existence of God. Similarly, Socrates, as he is presented in
the dialogues of Plato, normally proceeds by the method of
questioning everything in which people believe in order to
arrive at more adequate and certain definitions of what they
believe in. Yet it would be a great mistake to say that either
Descartes, Socrates, or Plato were sceptical philosophers.
They were in fact anything but philosophical sceptics. We
must carefully distinguish the methodological doubt of the
great philosophers, which is no more than a very useful
dialectical device, from the real doubts of the sceptical philosopher. The former employed the method of doubt during
the course of their arguments for the sake of arriving at more
certain conclusions. The latter may not do very much doubting in the actual course of his argument. His doubt is in his
conclusions, and that is what makes him a sceptic in the
proper sense of the word.

The more common and intelligent form of scepticism is
the kind of critical philosophy which we have already discussed. It attempts, as we have seen, to distinguish between
a sphere of discovery and enquiry in which knowledge is
possible and another sphere of discourse and enquiry in
which it is held to be unattainable.

This kind of philosopher is usually described as a positivist
when we think of him in relation to the kind of knowledge
which he regards as attainable by man, and as an agnostic
when we think of him in relation to his declaration that other

kinds of knowledge are unattainable. Thus, most sceptics are positivists and agnostics at the same time. Indeed, positivism and agnosticism are usually two differents aspects of the same philosophy.

Our criticism of this kind of philosophy has already been made clear. It misunderstands and misinterprets the consequences of the finitude of the human mind. Our conclusion was, when we discussed this question in the second chapter, that although we are incapable of knowing everything about anything because our minds are finite, yet we have no warrant whatever for believing that there is any reality which is entirely and in principle unknowable. In other words the positivist agnostic is much too positivist about that which he thinks that he can and does know, and much too agnostic about everything else. Reason will support neither the extreme optimism of his positivist mood nor the unqualified pessimism of the agnostic phase of his thought.

No doubt there have been some agnostics who cannot properly be called positivists. Such people will argue that the case for and against a metaphysical hypothesis like the existence of God is about evenly balanced, and that we have therefore no alternative but to suspend our judgment. This does not seem to me to be true. There are no positive arguments for atheism, corresponding to the positive arguments for theism. Indeed, it is difficult to see how there could be. A positive argument for a negative conclusion is in the very nature of the case a very rare thing. One is reminded of the story of the hedgehog who was discovered by a jack rabbit feverishly endeavoring to bury himself in the middle of the summer. "Whatever are you doing?" asked the jack rabbit,

"Haven't you heard," replied the hedgehog, "Congress has decided to investigate all the porcupines." "But you are not a porcupine," the jack rabbit assured him. "I know, but could I ever prove it?" moaned the hedgehog in despair. The moral of this story is perhaps political rather than metaphysical, but it does indicate the dialectical difficulty in which we find ourselves involved whenever we try to devise positive arguments for a purely negative conclusion.

But even if for the moment we accept the possibility that the arguments for theism and for atheism might conceivably be evenly balanced, is it really possible for us to suspend our judgment about a matter of this kind? The answer to this question must clearly be in the negative. It is never possible to suspend judgment about any question which involves action. To suspend judgment about a question which involves action is really to vacilate in indecision. Vacillation and indecision are quite different from a rational suspending of judgment. The question "Shall I believe in God or not?" is not really the purely theoretical question which it appears to be. "Shall I believe in God or not?" can and should be restated in another form. It really means "Shall I worship God or not?" For to believe in God without worshiping Him is not really to believe in *God* at all. Now clearly it is not possible to suspend judgment about a practical question like, "Shall I worship God?" The agnostic who sincerely supposes that he is suspending judgment on this matter is in fact, and perhaps without really wanting to, all the time coming down on the negative side. No doubt there are some purely theoretical questions about which we can and should suspend judgment, at all events for the moment. (For example, the question whether or not the planet Mars is inhabited.) But the question, "Shall I worship God or not?" is not a question of this kind. Here no true suspending of judgment is possible. How fortunate it is that the arguments for and against the existence of God are not really so evenly balanced as the agnostic supposes.

Atheism

Very few great philosophers have been dogmatic atheists, although a small minority have taught that God, or the gods, if He exists or they exist, is or are not concerned about us and that in consequence we need not in practice concern ourselves with Him or them. Normally, atheism takes the form of a criticism of such conceptions of God as are fashionable at any particular stage in the development of culture, and of such arguments as are put forward in an endeavor to prove the existence of God. As I have already suggested, such criticism may be of positive value. It is often the theists who provoke men to atheism by the unworthiness of their conceptions of God, and by the feebleness of the arguments with which they endeavor to support them. It would be very unwise for the religious man to dismiss all atheism as a negligible and irrelevant blasphemy. On the contrary, the best kind of atheism can teach us many salutary lessons. It warns us against forms of belief in God which are unworthy and sometimes more truly blasphemous than any kind of atheism can ever be. In a sense genuine atheism is a highly spiritual state of mind. The best kind of atheist is revolted and frustrated by ways of declaring the truth about God which quite plainly fail to meet the spiritual and intellectual needs of a spiritually and intellectually awakened man. In a way, indeed, the theist and the best kind of atheist are not so sharply opposed to each other as they seem. What the theist really asserts is not the total adequacy of any particular idea of God, not even his own idea, but the reality of God. What the atheist denies is not the reality of God—that, alas, is too far from his conscious experience for him even to deny it—but the adequacy of the ideas of God that are put before his mind by the believers. On the whole, indeed, atheism seems to me in every way the best alternative to theism. It is perhaps a pity that genuine atheism of the best kind is so very rare, for it has much to teach us of positive value.

Perhaps the most familiar form of atheism in the contemporary world is the Marxist variety. This can hardly be counted among the higher and more spiritual forms of atheism to which I have alluded, but it has two interesting characteristics which make it worth mentioning. It rejects theism not so much because it holds that the arguments for theism are defective or invalid—although, of course, it does do this—but because it regards belief in God and an ultimate destiny for man which "doth not yet appear" as an unhealthy belief which robs this present life of any consequence and value.

No doubt it is true that there have been some pervertedly pious people who have been led to the conclusion that the reality of God and the whole spiritual dimension of our experience make everything else comparatively unimportant. This is not, however, the outlook of the Bible or of historic Christianity as a whole. The belief that God made the world and that human life has an ultimate destiny and significance makes everything that happens here and now of supreme importance. It is, on the contrary, the belief that human existence is so to speak going nowhere, is a mere transitory phase in the evolution of the cosmos, which implies that life is objectively speaking, unimportant. If we are in fact going nowhere it cannot matter so very much precisely how we go. It is only if our journey has a specific destination that it becomes important to choose the right road and keep it in good repair. The idea that we shall be wiser and more resolute in dealing with the problems of this present life if we ignore its context and ultimate meaning is a quite incredible and totally invalid paradox. The true implication of the Christian gospel and the Christian interpretation of human existence is that the world really matters because it is God's world, that people really matter because they are God's children, and that the way they live their common life together in society and human history really matters because it is in society and human history that we must prepare ourselves for life in God's kingdom.

An even more notable feature of the specifically Marxist atheism—although one which it shares with several other kinds of atheism—is its way of introducing God, so to speak, under another name. In Marxism there is indeed some recognition of a force other than man and stronger than man which takes charge of human history and controls human destiny. This is what the Marxists call "the dialectic of history," a historical force or law of history operating within human history which ultimately determines the course of events. Often among communists we find something very like a kind of piety, which treats this dialectic of history as an almost personal force which is slowly but surely working its purpose out and which must be served by men with sincere devotion and self-sacrifice. It is this which gives to communist enthusiasm an almost religious or mystical quality, and it is on account of this reverent and obedient attitude toward the forces controlling history that some observers have been led to describe communism (rightly, in my view) as a kind of religion.

It is certainly true that we often find something very like a recognition of God among those who reject the name of God. Thus, among some purely naturalistic thinkers, nature and natural processes are taken to be the ultimately decisive force in life and are treated with the kind of reverence with which religious people approach God. The divine name is rejected but there is still some recognition of an objective controlling factor in human affairs which demands to be reverenced and obeyed. Of course, such conceptions of God are necessarily defective and idolatrous from the Christian point of view, but from the point of view of natural theology they are not without significance. They indicate that even some of the atheists feel compelled to recognize, although of course they would not admit it, the kind of intellectual need for an ultimate principle of reality and truth which leads those who are not prejudiced against the use of the word to declare the necessary existence of God.

Dualism

Some religious teachers, and perhaps a few philosophers, have been so profoundly impressed and influenced by the reality of evil that they have concluded that there exists not one God upon whom everything else that is not God depends, but two opposed ultimate principles, a principle of ultimate evil and a principle of ultimate good. The creation as we know it is a vast area of conflict between these two ultimate principles. This belief has taken many different forms, but by far its most common form throughout the Christian era has been a belief that it is the principle of ultimate evil who created the material universe, and that the God whom Christian men worship is the creator of spiritual reality alone. This easily leads to the conclusion that material and bodily existence is inherently evil and the source of all evil. The moral conflict is thus essentially a conflict within man between his spirituality and the demands and cravings of his fleshly nature.

In Christian history this kind of belief is usually called the Manichean heresy after Manichaeus, an ancient Persian teacher who was reared in the teaching of the Zoroastrian religion. For the first fifteen centuries or so of the Church's history heresies of this kind turned up again and again in many different places, and to some extent infiltrated the Church itself and influenced the thought and teaching of even rigidly orthodox defenders of the faith. During the last five hundred years, it appears to have died down, but in fact this kind of heretical teaching has manifested itself in a new form in the puritanism which has disfigured the life of so many Christian churches and sects since the Reformation. Puritanism is not, of course, explicitly Manichean in its teachings, but its general attitude toward life and its particular horror of the kinds of sin which are most obviously "the sins of the flesh" show that it has a profound affinity with the old Manichean heresy.

We may trace in this kind of thinking two basic errors, one theological, one philosophical. The theological mistake is that of supposing that the root of our sin is our physical or fleshly nature. This is a grave error. All sin is by nature not a physical but a spiritual process. Or, in other words, only spiritual beings are capable of sin. Even the sins which look like "sins of the flesh" are in fact sins in which a spiritual being abuses the physical nature and potentialities entrusted to his spiritual care. Thus, for example, there is no "drink evil." A physical thing like a drink cannot conceivably be evil. The crux of the evil of drunkenness is the abuse of drink, the greedy and intemperate use of something which is in itself neither good nor evil. Similarly if a wife murders her husband by poisoning him with arsenic, we should not dream of calling this the "arsenic evil." It is the spiritual woman, not the arsenic, who is guilty, and she has misused arsenic in order to inherit her husband's fortune, or for the sake of marrying some other man.

If, however, we take a New Testament point of view of the basic moral issues of human existence, we shall see that the so-called sins of the flesh are not even the worst sins. In the New Testament it is pride and lack of love rather than over-indulgence and sensuality which utterly destroy and pervert human souls, and so it is that even the publicans and the harlots go into the Kingdom of Heaven before the highly respectable Pharisees.

The Old Testament tells the same story. Thus in the great

113

myth of the Fall of Man which we find in the second and third chapters of Genesis, the serpent does not lure Eve to destruction by tempting her sensuality, by telling her that the forbidden fruit has an exquisite taste of which she must not allow herself to be cheated by the Divine prohibition. On the contrary, he tempts her spirituality. "If you show yourself strong enough to disobey God," he tells her in effect, "you will become like God, sharing his knowledge of good and evil and transcending the contrast between the two." This perverted desire of the spiritual creature to place himself on equality with God is indeed the sin of sins, and the heart and root of all sin. Yet it has nothing to do with the fact that we possess a physical nature, for it is only possible in a spiritual being. We do not sin with the lowest part of ourselves, but with the highest part of ourselves. Indeed, so far as we know, we are the only beings whom God has placed in this world who are even capable of sinning, and it is because we are capable of sin that we are fit for salvation. Manicheanism and puritanism—of course they differ in many ways, but fundamentally, I believe, they are agreed—are thus completely mistaken about the nature and cause of evil, and this mistake lies at the root of all their other errors.

The philosophical error is perhaps the more obvious. If God is indeed that primordial being upon whom everything that is not God depends for its existence, then there cannot be two gods. If there are two gods or two ultimate principles of being, then in fact neither of them is God, for the existence of each of them is limited by the parallel existence of the other. To acknowledge more than one God is in fact, as the early Christians saw so clearly, to be an atheist. Once we properly understand what the word God really means it becomes obvious to us that there can only be one God, only one ultimate creative principle upon whom everything else depends for its existence. Even more obvious is the difficulty of seeing how, if there are two creators who do not collaborate together in harmony but are eternally hostile to each other, their respective creations can fuse together in what at all events appears to be one world or one universe. After all on very strict Manichean principles each individual human being, a union of body and spirit, is partly the creature of the principle of evil and partly the creature of the principle of good. If we interpret him in this way how can man conceivably be one creature? It is true that fallen man is aware of conflict within himself; but if the dualistic philosophy is true, this conflict is an ultimately irreconcilable one, not one from which he could hope to be redeemed by any conceivable redemptive act of God.

Evil is certainly a problem, but it cannot conceivably be interpreted and understood in such terms as these. Christian theism sees the mystery of evil as essentially the mystery of its presence in a world created by the just and loving and utterly righteous God. No doubt the mystery must always remain. The problem is not the problem of understanding the mystery, but the problem of learning how to live with evil creatively, so that faith shall not be confounded, hope dissipated and charity turned into bitterness and hate by the evil which enters into our experience. This is the problem which we see so triumphantly solved by Jesus Christ in His incarnate life, and in particular at the moment of its great climax upon the Cross. The only way in which we can begin to enter into the heart of the mystery with some kind of understanding is to see the possibility of evil as somehow inherent within the possibility of good. We have already remarked that it is only because man is capable of sin that he is fit for salvation. Inherent in the very nature of finite spiritual being, in its splendid dignity and tremendous potentialities, is the possibility of its self-perversion. Sin and evil are, so to speak, by-products of finite spiritual existence. Not to create beings capable of sin would be not to create beings fit for salvation. In the divine mind, clearly, the risk was worth running and the price worth paying. Once we have learned to interpret evil in this way, we have no alternative but to acquiesce in the divine verdict.

Pluralism

Pluralism is the belief that the universe is composed of many realities, all of them equally ultimate and equally real. Ancient pagan polytheism, the belief in the existence of many different gods and goddesses, is one form of pluralism, but there are many modern forms of it which recognize, logically enough, no divinities at all. Thus, there is a personal or spiritual pluralism which believes that the ultimate reality is simply a plurality of personal existences. There is also a scientific, possibly materialistic, pluralism, which believes that the ultimate realities are the units of matter or force, whatever they may be called, in terms of which physical science interprets all physical phenomena. But although pluralism may exist in many different forms, the basic philosophical difficulty remains always the same. In effect pluralism means that there are many distinct realities existing side by side with one another and in some sort of relationship with one another, but the relationship of different things to one another is not something external or added on to their own individual nature. The different things of which the world is composed need one another and depend upon one another, and the existence of one is unintelligible apart from the existence of others. Thus a cow is distinct from the air that she breathes, the cud that she chews, the water that she drinks, and the parents who brought her into the world. Yet apart from the air, the cud, the water, and the parent bull and the parent cow, she could not exist or even have come into existence. In other words all the distinct entities of which our world is composed are what we have called contingent realities. They do not explain their own existence; they cannot account for their own existence; and therefore their reality cannot be the ultimate reality of which we need ask no further questions. They are real but not ultimately real, and the mere affirmation of their reality cannot possibly constitute a satisfactory account of their reality. If they were all of them ultimately real, that is ultimately independent of one another, we could never account for the plain fact of their immediate dependence on one another, nor for the fact that they live a common life in one universe. Philosophically speaking, pluralism is perhaps the least satisfactory of all the known alternatives to theism.

Pantheism

At the opposite end of the scale from pluralism is monism, a philosophy which usually implies, or is at least closely connected with, pantheism in religion. According to this philoso-

phy the universe, far from being composed of a vast collection of separate entities, is in fact a single spiritual being,
and what appear to be separate beings and things are in fact
no more than different phases or aspects of this one being's
activity and self-manifestation. Just as for pluralism the
reality is the many, so that in consequence pluralism cannot
explain the unity of the many, so for monism and pantheism
the reality is the one, so that these doctrines cannot explain
the diversity and plurality which meets us on the level of
immediate experience. (Theism, of course, explains this
problem of the one and the many by saying that both are
real in their own form and degree: the necessary being or
ultimate creative principle is one, and the contingent beings
or created and dependent, finite realities are many. In these
terms we can indeed make sense of the ultimate unity of the
many, and the diversity of reality at the level of our own experience.)

Pantheism identifies God with everything that exists, interpreted as constituting one single composite or collective being. Thus, God is another name for everything. There are
two difficulties about this view, one ethical, the other logical
or metaphysical. If God is simply the totality of all being
considered as a unity, if He is in everything and everything
is in Him, then none of the distinctions we make between
different things and forms of experience can have any ultimate meaning. All is God, and all things are lost and confounded together in the dark night of the divine being. So
far as many of the distinctions with which we are familiar
are concerned, this would no doubt not matter very much,
but there are some distinctions which we cannot make intel-

ligently or intelligibly unless we suppose that they have ultimate meaning and validity. Consider, for example, our
ethical distinctions between good and evil (*e.g.* between
justice and injustice) and the philosophical distinctions apart
from which many of the highest forms of ethical experience
would be impossible (*e.g.* the distinction between different
persons which is necessary if the great values which we find
in personal experience, faithfulness, trust, love, and so on,
are to have any ultimate meaning or worth). If God is indeed
identical with everything, then injustice is as divine as justice, and the distinction between persons who trust, love,
and sacrifice themselves for one another is an ultimate illusion. Some pantheists and monists talk glibly about a god
who is *beyond* good and evil, but, in fact, if the words good
and evil have any real meaning it is impossible to be *beyond*
good and evil.

There are three possibilities in relation to the distinction
between ultimate good and ultimate evil. Either we hold fast
to the good and abjure the evil, or we surrender to evil and
isolate ourselves from the good, or we merely ignore the
whole distinction as unimportant and irrelevant. Of these
three possibilities the last is in fact the most evil of all. It is
not possible to be *beyond* good and evil but it is, alas, possible to sink so low as to be *beneath* good and evil, and this
is the worst and most depraved form of spiritual existence.
The god of pantheism is in fact beneath good and evil in this
sense, lower and more depraved even than the traditional
idea of Satan, neither embodying the good and existing as the
fount of all goodness, nor recognizing the good sufficiently
to war against it, but existing from all eternity in sheer indif-

ference to or total ignorance of the basic conception which establishes the possibility of the higher forms of spiritual experience. The god of pantheism is in fact not really god at all, but simply a kind of personification of everything in general.

Pantheism in practice sometimes seems a warm and attractive thing because it is akin to the spirit of some of the highest and noblest types of poetry, for example, much of the best poetry of William Wordsworth. This is the kind of poetry in which men interpret their aesthetic enjoyment of the spectacle of nature and their feeling of our kinship as fellow creatures with the natural order in a religious way. It is certainly true that for many men the enjoyment of the spectacle of the beauty of nature is an occasion of genuine religious experience. "The heavens declare the glory of God; and the firmament showeth His handiwork." This kind of poetry can be found even in the Bible itself. But it is a manifest intellectual confusion if we suppose that because the spectacle of the beauty of nature often moves the human spirit to adoration and worship, that it is therefore the beauty of nature itself which is adored and worshiped. If we intensely enjoy the music of Beethoven, it is Beethoven himself rather than the music whom we admire and praise. The apparent pantheism of so many of the greatest nature poets is due to an intellectual error of this kind. Our own detection of the error should not, of course, prevent us from enjoying and being spiritually edified by the poetry. Pantheism as a philosophy and religious doctrine is not any less preposterous because a great deal of pantheistic sounding poetry is noble and inspiring. The great poet justifies his existence by the beauty of his poetry. We ought not to require of him that he should necessarily be at the same time a great philosopher and a reliable theological guide.

Deism

This alternative to theism is now almost, perhaps quite, abandoned and forgotten, but we may mention it here for the sake of completeness. According to deism, God created the world but, having created it, He interests Himself no further in the course of its existence. We have already remarked that this theory was very largely sustained by a belief that the universe is a perfect machine. The celestial mechanic started it going, but it is so perfectly designed and manufactured that it requires no subsequent intervention on the part of its designer and creator. The difficulty about this analogy, as we have seen, is that this is not in fact the way in which any of the machines with which we are acquainted behave. A greater difficulty is that this theory requires us to believe in a totally completed creation. It reflects and depends upon a scientific picture and interpretation of the universe which was only possible in pre-Darwinian times. That is one reason why deism nowadays makes no appeal to any kind of philosopher at all. Religiously speaking the idea of a god who cared enough about the world to bring it into existence, but not sufficiently to concern himself with it any further is quite incredible, and it would require more simple faith than most of us have at our disposal even to imagine what it would be like to profess so ridiculous a creed.

We have attempted no more in this chapter than a very brief and summary discussion indeed, but we have at least been able to indicate that the achievements of natural theology in what I have called its negative mood are by no means unimportant. When we look at the possible alternatives to theism—which are also and equally, of course, alternatives to one another—they do not appear to be a particularly impressive collection. I have ventured on the perhaps somewhat questionable opinion that atheism is the best and most respectable of them, if only because it takes the question of the existence of God with radical seriousness. Nevertheless, atheism cannot stand by itself. It amounts, after all, to no more than a declaration that theism is not true. It requires to be supplemented, therefore, by some alternative account of the universe. This can hardly take the form of either dualism, pantheism or deism. In fact, therefore, atheism is almost certainly driven to some form of pluralism, so that in most cases the objections to pluralism are also additional objections to atheism, and the objections to pluralism seem to me quite decisive and insuperable.

It is possible for a philosopher to hold that the arguments in favor of a theistic philosophy are not absolutely convincing beyond all possibility of rational doubt, but I think that he may well be constrained to admit that at least the case for philosophical theism is immeasurably stronger than the case which can be made out for any alternative to theism. If we can indeed say that either A or B or C or D must be true; that A is probably, although perhaps not quite certainly, true;

that B, C, and D are either very improbable or altogether out of the question; then surely we are justified in concluding that for all practical purposes we may assume that A is so very probably true that its high degree of probability is in effect almost indistinguishable from sheer certainty?

CHAPTER FIVE

A THEOLOGY OF NATURE?

We remarked at the end of our first chapter that the very conception of a theology of nature raises the whole question of the scope and logical structure of theology itself. It is not the purpose of this chapter to supply a theology of nature in even the barest outline. I regard the idea of a theology of nature as no more than a project. It cannot be claimed that Christian thought has ever produced a developed theology of nature in the past, nor that it is actively engaged in producing such a theology now. We have to ask ourselves whether a theology of nature is a feasible theological project? What kind of speculative doctrine a theology of nature, if we had one, would be? And what would be the value of a theology of nature, if we had one, in relation to current controversies and perplexities?

Two Kinds of Theological Thinking

The historian of Christian theology may usefully distinguish between two distinct types of theological thought (research and speculation) that easily harden into two different kinds of theology. One kind of theology confines itself to the specialized study and interpretation of what we may call specifically theological data, theological things and experiences in the narrower sense of the word. This kind of theology tends to be existentialist and redemptionist in its tone. Its first emphasis is upon man's experience of being a sinner, of the inescapable consequences of sin, and of man's powerlessness to help or save himself or to surmount the crisis of his own existence. Its second emphasis is on the way in which God in and through Jesus Christ has come to man's rescue and done that for him which he cannot do for himself.

In this kind of theology the doctrine of atonement, redemption, or salvation (all these classical theological terms are concerned with the same empirical reality) is the primary theme of the Christian gospel, and the basic or architectonic idea of Christian theology. It is the architectonic idea because this particular type of theological thought tends to answer all other theological problems in terms of the doctrine of redemption. Thus, in classical theology, all enquiries which seek to answer such questions as who or what was Jesus Christ, and what do we mean when we claim that He is God-made-man are called Christological enquiries. They seek to determine the *logos* or rationale of the Christ, to make sense of the Church's experience of and attitude toward its Lord. Now the kind of theology which we are trying to describe has its own characteristic way of handling this question. It seeks to understand the mystery of the person of Jesus Christ through the study of what we know of the work of Christ. Christ, as men know him in the Church, is the Saviour and redeemer of sinners. We may therefore ask ourselves what kind of being must a historical figure possess if He is to be the Saviour of sinners?

In order to answer this question, we have to consider the nature of sin and the needs of sinners, and thus arrive at a kind of mental picture of the kind of saviour that sinners require. In this way we arrive at our understanding of the incarnation. The incarnation is the coming into the world of the kind of being who would be able to save us from our sins.

There is nothing peculiarly evangelical or post-reformation about this kind of theology. On the contrary, we discover similar processes of reasoning even in the early classical period of the growth of Christian theology which we call patristic. Thus, the fourth century heretic Apolinarius taught that Christ did not assume a complete human nature, but only a partial, outward-seeming human nature. The orthodox objected that if this were so, He could not be the Saviour of the whole of our human nature, because what He did not assume He could not save. In order, in other words, to save human nature, the Christ must unite the whole human nature to God. The point of this objection was that those who made it assumed that whatever else we know or do not know about the Christ we are at least certain that He is the Saviour of the whole human nature.

This kind of theology has many advantages to recommend it. It has the virtue of keeping very close to the basic Christian religious experience and to the actual way in which the Church preaches and must preach the gospel. It reduces to the barest minimum the difference of atmosphere between what the Church says when it proclaims the gospel and what it says in its more intellectual setting forth of its theology. Many theologians, particularly those who like to call themselves evangelical, desire their theology to sound as much like their preaching as possible. This is understandable, because nowadays most theologians are clergymen (it may be questioned whether this is not really a misfortune for the Church) and most clergymen are expected to be preachers, or at least to preach very frequently (which is perhaps not quite the same thing). This kind of theology has also a further advantage. Since the whole of its thinking is based upon a single point of departure from within the Christian experience, and one particular doctrine or doctrinal theme provides it with a single architectonic idea, it can easily be expressed in a highly systematic, streamlined way.

Nevertheless, it has certain disadvantages. There is much in God's creation, and in human life and experience, with which this kind of theology does not seem to be concerned. It succeeds in making theology appear systematic, rounded, and complete only at the cost of drastically narrowing its scope. Nor is it quite clear that its point of departure is in fact a possible or proper point of departure at all. It begins with man's existential experience and his certainty that he is a sinner. But can man really explain what he means when he declares himself to be a sinner without some reference to a doctrine of creation and the purpose of God in creating man, in the light of which he is able to perceive that he is in fact a sinner? Sin is presumably a failure on the part of man

127

to be what he is meant to be and to become what he is meant to become, a tragic falling short of his own proper stature. Sin is the failure of the whole human race to occupy its own proper level and fulfil its own proper function in the created order. But how can we say this unless we have some idea of what it is that we are falling short of, what it is that we are failing to become? In other words, our experience of sin and our doctrinal declaration that we are all sinners presupposes what is from the logical point of view a more fundamental doctrine. It presupposes the doctrine of the creation of the world by God as the instrument of His loving purpose, a purpose fulfilled in the perfect humanity of Christ by the power of God, and therefore in principle a purpose which may be fulfilled in us despite our sins in so far as our humanity is joined to and becomes one with Christ's humanity in the life of the Church.

In saying this we have pointed the way toward a rather different kind of theology. From this new point of view it will appear that the doctrine of creation is logically more fundamental than the doctrine of redemption, and that the problem of the Incarnation—the question who or what was Jesus Christ—must be answered in terms of the doctrine of the creation as well as in terms of the doctrine of redemption. We now see that the perfect humanity of Christ is the living embodiment in human history of the purpose of God in creating human nature and human history. The Christ reveals to us not only the fact of human redemption but the purpose of the creation. From this point of view we see that the Christ is a cosmic figure, the very crown and summit of the creation, the logos or principle of creation which was in the beginning, the "last thing" or principle of judgment which shall triumph at the consummation of all things. He is for us the first and the last, and in Him all things consist.

This leads us to a kind of theology for which the basic, architectonic, theological ideas are those of creation and incarnation. This is often called incarnational theology, and it is one which from Hooker onward has been the peculiar possession and characteristic of the theological thought and speculation of the Anglican communion, distinguishing Anglical theology rather sharply from that traditional in the Lutheran and Reformed churches.

In pre-reformation theology we find, side by side with each other, tendencies in both the redemptionist and incarnationalist directions, but no very clear decision between the two. In the middle ages the whole question was raised in a very simple but striking way: Would Christ have been born among men if men had not sinned? After a very balanced discussion of the whole issue, St. Thomas Aquinas came down rather tentatively on the negative, redemptionist side, although it is true to say that on the whole the theology of Aquinas tends to be incarnationalist. In this context, he argues that all that we certainly know is that men have sinned and that Christ has become incarnate, and to suppose that there may have been an incarnation without any sin is to venture into realms of unprofitable speculation.

Duns Scotus, however, took the other side. He held that the purpose of God in creating the world and mankind was one which from the beginning envisaged the incarnation. The purpose of God in creating the world and mankind is not one which is fulfilled in the mere act of creation, but rather one which will be fulfilled at the consummation of all things. The Incarnation is thus, for him, necessary to the fulfilment of the whole plan of creation because the purpose of God in the creation is not fulfilled in the world and in the drama of human existence as we know it, but rather in the Kingdom of God which will issue out of it.

The position maintained by Duns Scotus has for us two very important advantages, of the second of which Duns Scotus, himself, was quite unaware. In the first place, it is closer to the New Testament. The New Testament does indeed speak again and again of Christ as the Saviour and redeemer of sinners, but elsewhere, particularly in the fourth gospel and in the Epistles to the Colossians and the Ephesians, it presents Him as the cosmic Christ, the crown and fulfilment of the whole creation and the clue to the meaning of the creation. More than that, Duns Scotus's view is in harmony with the eschatological emphasis which we find running right through the New Testament. In these eschatological passages Christ is repeatedly presented, not merely as the redeemer of sinners here and now, but as the last thing, as the final principle of judgment and victory in and through whom the whole purpose of the creation will be accomplished and the whole meaning of it laid bare.

But if this incarnationalist kind of theology has the advantage of being so much closer to Holy Scripture as a whole (the redemptionist kind of theology, at least since Luther, has always tended to lay special emphasis on certain favorite New Testament passages, chiefly Pauline, and to allow the rest of the New Testament to fall into comparative obscurity) it has also the secondary advantage of fitting in, very illuminatingly, with much that we now know about the processes which characterize the life of the universe.

The New Testament and the kind of incarnationalist theology which we find in Scotus knew nothing about the concept of evolution, and yet they are both evolutionist in their outlook. Evolution suggests that the real meaning of a process is not to be found in the way in which it begins but in the way in which it consummates itself. The eschatological passages in the New Testament suggest precisely the same doctrine. The concept of evolution suggests that in a very real sense the creation of the world is not yet finished; the process of creation is still going on. The kind of incarnationalist theology which we find in Duns Scotus suggests very much the same thing. For him, as we have seen, the incarnation is not only necessary to the process of redeeming man but it is also necessary to the process of creating man, a process which will only be consummated in the Kingdom of God.

Until very recently, almost all theologians were agreed (and almost all non-theologians also) that the creation of the world had been completed. The Christian theologian tended also to believe that the human part of the creation at least had been spoiled by sin, and the purpose of the creation to that extent obstructed or even nullified, so that man stood in need of a redemption which would restore to the creation its original integrity and visible conformity to the divine purpose. This kind of attitude, as we have noticed, was out of harmony with the eschatological outlook which we find everywhere in the New Testament. But on the whole it is true, and not too harsh to say, that for many hundreds of years Christian theologians of all schools of thought have contrived to ignore, or at least push very much into the background, that eschatological outlook which is so very much in the foreground of the New Testament itself.

We must, however, not be too hard on the theologians. They tended to assume that the creation was finished very largely because most of the best science of their own day assumed the same thing. Darwin, in other words, has rendered a great service to theological thinking, and made it possible for us to apprehend shades of meaning in the New Testament which generations of our predecessors scarcely noticed.

Our realization of the importance of this conception of an unfinished creation is clearly expressed in a letter written by the late Archbishop Temple shortly before his death:

What we must completely get away from is the notion that the world as it now exists is a rational whole; we must think of its unity not by the analogy of a picture, of which all the parts exist at once, but by the analogy of a drama where, if it is good enough, the full meaning of the first scene only becomes apparent in the final curtain; and we are in the middle of this. Consequently the world as we see it is strictly unintelligible. We can only have faith that it will become intelligible when the Divine purpose, which is the explanation of it, is accomplished. Theologically, this is a greater emphasis on eschatology.[1]

[1] F. A. Iremonger, *William Temple* (New York: Oxford), pp. 537-8. Quoted by Dorothy Emmett in the chapter which she contributed to this volume. Used by permission of the publisher.

From the point of view of such an approach to theology as this, it will easily be seen that Christ is interpreted as much more than the Saviour of sinners. He is indeed the Saviour of sinners, but He is also the clue to the meaning and purpose of the whole universe. Hence, for this incarnationalist theology the scope of theology, its proper sphere of interest, comprehends the entire creation. This observation gives us a catholic theology, in a slightly new sense of the word catholic.

This catholic theology is very far from being the theology of all catholic theologians, although it is probably true that almost all catholic theologians, as distinct from evangelical theologians, tend in this direction. This kind of theology is catholic in the sense we use when we say that a man's literary or artistic tastes are catholic, meaning that his mind is unrestricted by prejudice, unmarred by blind spots, and wide open to every variety of literary or artistic experience and value. This theology is catholic because it is, in principle, an attempt to give a theological account and interpretation of everything that is or will be. It is only from the point of view of such a theology as this that a specific theology of nature is a feasible project.

Perhaps one word of warning may be timely and proper before we conclude this particular part of our discussion. We have been talking about the distinction between two different kinds of theology. Controversies that stem from these can be very profound and far reaching, and they may sharply divide us from one another on the intellectual level. But let us notice that these are not really controversies about religion at all; they are controversies about theology and theological procedure. We can differ about such questions on the intellectual level and yet remain at one with one another on that profounder level where we confess our faith and worship our God.

Theological differences need not, indeed should not, involve religious differences or ecclesiastical divisions. The redemptionist type of theologian believes in the incarnation; the incarnationalist dare never forget that he is himself a redeemed sinner. The controversies between us are concerned with the manner and scope of theological thinking. They are not controversies about the substance of the Gospel itself. There we can agree in a common act of faith.

Nevertheless, these theological issues, although certainly not the profoundest issues, are grave and important. Our theologizing will do much to determine the way in which we present and communicate the Christian gospel to the world and the way in which Christian thought will relate itself to the thinking and the doubting and the self-questioning of men in the world. In a world in which there are many intellectuals to be saved, and in which the intellectuals fashion climates of opinion by which even the minds of non-intellectuals are often decisively influenced, the precise form which the Christian intellectualism (another name for the Church's theology) assumes and the terms in which it asserts itself are matters of crucial importance. They are closely related to the success or failure which attend the Church's efforts to fulfil its evangelistic functions and to discharge its evangelical responsibilities.

134

Theology and Science

Theology has usually been related to science in the setting of the rather hackneyed and dreary "science *vs.* religion" controversy. The main aim of the Christian apologist, when thinking and speaking in this context, is to show that the kind of truth which we find in Christianity is not really incompatible with the kind of truth which science supplies. He may try to do this, for example, by arguing that the evolutionary account of the growth of the universe and the emergence of man are quite in harmony with the essential point and teaching of the colorful poetic myth with which the Book of Genesis opens. Alternatively, he may try to show that theology and religion answer questions different from those which science answers and that they are concerned with phases or aspects of reality or experience different from those with which the scientist is concerned.

There is indeed much of value that can be said along these lines, but it is doubtful if we can ever get to the very heart of the matter in this way. The trouble is not so much that some of the things which the natural scientist sees and teaches may at first sight appear to contradict or to be out of harmony with essential religious and theological teachings. These are but minor frictions, which will almost certainly be lessened and thus ultimately disappear in the course of time, as our knowledge increases and our analysis becomes more profound. The real tension between science and religion, and this particularly from the point of view of those working or interested in science, is the difference between the logical categories and methods employed

135

in these two different fields. The scientist is apt to feel, as he peruses and considers some work of philosophical or theological thought, that its standards of rational judgment and its methods of seeking truth, even perhaps its criterion of truth itself, are very different from those with which he is familiar in his own sphere of research. If there is any truth in religion in general, or in Christianity in particular, it seems to him to be a kind of truth which he can never reach by employing the methods he employs in the sciences. He is apt to demand that it be possible for him to make sense of Christianity in the same kind of way that he is accustomed to make sense of the data of his own science. Thus, he complains when he finds that this cannot be done and feels that there is apparently no making any sense of Christianity at all.

This raises the question of the relation of the human mind to the logical categories and methods which it employs on different occasions, and in relation to different types of problems. There are two possible approaches to this issue, one holding in effect that the human mind is and ought to be enslaved by its categories and methods, the other holding that the human mind is free in relation to them.

The first approach we may call the dogmatic one. According to this view there are certain categories and methods which constitute the very essence of reason itself. The only valid kind of thinking is the kind of thinking which employs these categories; all other modes of thought are invalid and ultimately meaningless. This approach lays down precisely what these categories and methods are, and gives us what purports to be a universal definition of the very nature of science (*i.e.* that science is a mental discipline which thinks in terms of *x*-categories and employs *y*-methods to the total exclusion of all others). In other words science is known and recognized neither by the purposes which it serves, nor by the motives which inspire it, nor by the kind of result that it achieves, but by the logic and rules of procedure to which it conforms.

The worst consequence of this view is that it fails to do justice to the differences among the many distinct sciences, differences which are dictated by the great variety of the subject matter of the sciences concerned. This habit of dogmatizing about the categories leads to a demand that all the sciences should ideally look alike, that is, that they should all possess the same logical shape. Because of the tremendous success and prestige of the physical sciences in the modern world, this usually takes the form of a demand that all sciences, if they are to be acknowledged as sciences, should resemble the physical sciences in their logical structure. This cramping dogma has often made things difficult in the biological sciences which, in the view of many workers in this field, require categories, for example the category of purpose, with which the physical sciences can dispense. In what are called the social sciences, the necessity of making all "scientific" enquiries look as much like physics as possible has lead to distortion, and often ridiculous results. Those, like the so-called logical positivists, who are most ruthless in asserting this dogmatic view of the scientific categories, and who insist on working them out to their last logical consequences, usually hold that speculative disciplines like philosophy and theology can have no meaning at all.

There is a very obvious, although in some ways rather subtle, initial objection to any view of this kind. The belief that only the categories and methods employed in the physical sciences have rational validity cannot itself be discovered by employing the methods of physics and it cannot be asserted within the terms of its categories. There is no scientific way of demonstrating the truth of the proposition, or of verifying the hypothesis, that the scientific categories and methods of the physical sciences are the only rational ones. The assertion is thus a dogmatic presupposition, presumably presupposed and asserted under the influence of some kind of belief that without such a presupposition faith in the validity of science is impossible.

Our second possible interpretation of man's relation to his categories calls such a belief into question. From this point of view, the hallmark of truly scientific procedure is the devising of logical categories and methods appropriate to the subject matter being studied. Its emphasis is upon the resilience and flexibility of the reason, its mastery of its categories, its freedom to employ one set of categories in one sphere of discourse and quite a different set in another.

We catch perhaps the first glimpse of the possibility of man's freedom in relation to his categories in the third of Kant's three great *Critiques*. In his first *Critique*, Kant had seemed to assume that the categories of pure reason are the basic, elemental categories of the human mind, the same wherever men are men, so that the categories we use in one sphere of discourse are necessarily the categories which we must use in any other. In his third *Critique,* however, Kant faces fairly and squarely the possibility that in the biological sciences the very nature of the subject matter may demand the employment of categories other than those which are required by the subject matter of mathematical physics. At this point, he speculates rather tentatively that man may after all have a certain freedom in relation to his categories, that there may be several sets of categories among which we may validly choose in accordance with their appropriateness to the particular kind of intellectual problem with which we are wrestling.

Since Kant's time the probability that this may indeed be so has been heavily reinforced by the discovery that even in the realm of mathematics important alternatives exist and real choices may and must be made. Thus, from Euclid to the second half of the nineteenth century men knew and employed only one geometry. This geometry assumed that space had the character of a large, three dimensional box. Today, we know that many alternative geometries are possible, and one of them, not very happily entitled the geometry of curved space, has assumed great scientific importance because of its employment in relativity physics.

This use of the so-called geometry of curved space in contemporary physics must not be misunderstood. The point is not that we used to believe that space is boxy but that modern science has now discovered that space is really curved. I remember a woman once saying to me, "What's all this nonsense about space being curved? Look at it; you can see for yourself that it's nothing of the kind." This is to mis-understand the nature and function of a geometry, which does not reproduce facts but interprets relations.

Space is neither curved nor boxy, but spacial relations can be validly interpreted and described in terms of several distinct geometries. Which geometry we in fact choose to employ will depend upon the precise purposes which we have in mind. Thus, for example, even in this age of relativity-physics, the land surveyor still employs a three dimensional geometry because this is the kind of geometry which suits his purposes. Historically speaking, in fact, three dimensional geometry was essentially a geometry for land surveying. It was the experience of the Egyptians in building the pyramids that lay behind the Euclidian geometry. It was only when the physicists stopped being universe surveyors *à la* Newton and became interpreters of physical events *à la* Einstein that the classical geometry proved inadequate and had to be replaced by another. But we must always bear in mind that *neither* geometry is *true*. A geometry is no more than a set of categories, a tool of analysis, useful in one context and less useful, perhaps even useless, in another.

Thus, even a study of trends of development in the physical sciences during the last half century supports a belief in man's rational freedom in relation to his categories. Once such a point of view is established, we shall cease to require or expect that the kind of truth given to us in Christianity and Christian theology must, if rational men are to accept it, necessarily be a kind of truth which can be discovered by the methods which the sciences employ or must be expressed in terms of the categories to which a scientific

140

training accustoms the scientific mind. We shall not expect or demand either that science shall be able to make sense of Christianity or that it must express Christianity's meaning within the limits of its own highly specialized terminology.

There is, however, a valid demand which may be made from the other side of the fence. It ought to be possible for Christian theology, using its own categories and methods, to interpret and make sense of the fruitfulness and success of the scientific method, when employed in the service of its own proper purposes and in relation to its own highly speccialized subject matter. This is the problem to which what I have called a theology of nature must address itself. It must answer two very fundamental questions: How is it that created reality is, among many other things, a possible and proper subject for successful scientific scrutiny and analysis? It must also answer an additional, although closely related question: How is it that man is the kind of being who, among many other things, is capable of analyzing, and to some extent knowing, created reality by the employment of a scientific method which he has himself devised? Such problems must be solved by theology in terms of its own doctrine of creation and its own doctrine of man.

I believe that the clue to the solution of these problems is to be found in the Biblical assertion that man is made in the express image of the God who has created everything that is not God. The possibility and success of science points, more clearly than anything else within the limits of our natural experience, to the fundamental kinship between the Creator who called the facts of our experience into being and the creatures who, alone among all the creatures, possess this awe-inspiring capacity to probe and understand them.

The fact that man is capable of achieving a scientific knowledge and understanding of the world in which he finds himself is, after all, something of a problem. So far as we know no other creature of the world is capable of attaining scientific knowledge or anything remotely resembling it. In a very real sense scientific man in knowing and interpreting the world in his own scientific way stands over against the world, distinguishes himself from the world, we might almost say transcends the world. Again, in seeking for and to some extent discovering a sheer objective truth about the world in the course of his scientific researches, when we see them conducted with the highest degree of intellectual integrity, man as scientist transcends both the peculiarities of his own private psychology and the interests of the social group to which he belongs; that is, he pushes beyond the possibility of mere rationalization or ideology. In a very real sense man as scientist transcends even himself. Such a transcendence of one's environment and one's selfhood is only a possibility for what theology calls a spiritual being. The very fact of scientific achievement is one which calls for a theological account and interpretation of man. Science is in fact an inherently spiritual activity; it is itself a form, and a very high form, of spirituality.

Indeed, one of the intellectual developments which most of all menaces science and scientific activity from within contemporary thought is the widespread tendency among those thinkers who are particularly impressed with the importance of science and its successes to conceive of what they call a purely scientific account of man himself, which may easily and paradoxically suggest that man is not in fact the kind of being who is capable of becoming a scientist. According to many writers, a really scientific view of man must interpret him as being utterly conditioned and determined by the world in which he lives and by the unalterable peculiarities of his own private psychology. Such a being would not be capable of the objectivity, the intellectual integrity and the transcendence of his world and his condition which the scientific ideal demands of its devotees and practitioners. What science really requires and implies is not the kind of picture of man that is given in what is sometimes called the Scientific World View, but the theological picture of man as the child of God whose mind is adequate to the task of knowing and interpreting the world because he is made in the image of the Creator of the world.

Again, the success of science is really a verification of its conviction that this world is the kind of world which can only be known by empirical means. We cannot know or interpret the world by any kind of pure, deductive, rational analysis which attempts to decide what the world in the nature of the case must be like. In the long run we can only find out what things are like by observing them carefully and experimenting with them resourcefully. But what kind of world is it which can only be known scientifically by using the empirical method? The answer seems pretty clear: The world which can only be known by the empirical method is the world as it is conceived and defined in the terms of the Christian theology, the created, contingent world which does not have to be but merely happens to be, which might conceivably have been otherwise than it is, which might quite conceivably not have been at all. The success of the scientific method thus contributes in a most striking way to the verification of the metaphysical account of the world which we find in classical Christian theology. Indeed, it is perhaps no accident that the scientific method as we now know it was first invented and devised in a mental climate which was dominated by classical Christian theology. The philosophical justification of the attitude toward the world adopted by the first pioneers of modern science, and the methods which they devised in order to seek the truth about it, was the account of the world given by the theologians. The pioneers of modern science thus correctly diagnosed the logical and methodological consequences of the Christian doctrine of creation.

The proper way of relating theology to scientific thought, then, is not to attempt to show, desperately (and ultimately in vain) that Christianity is, after all, something to which the scientific mind can do justice in its own terms, but rather that the scientist himself and the phenomenal success of his science is something to which the theologian can and must do justice in his own proper terms. The honest scientist is mistaken if he supposes that he cannot with intellectual integrity accept Christianity unless he can somehow force its truth into the mold of his own scientific categories. What his intellectual honesty really requires, and must demand, is not that his science should be capable of interpreting and apprehending his Christianity but that his Christianity should be able to make sense of his science. Thus, the proper context in which to relate theology to modern science is not that of the stale "science *vs.* religion" controversy, but that of the theology of nature, which we can now see to be indispensable, not only for apologetic purposes, but also for the intellectual completeness of our theology itself.

The Analogy Between Theology and Science

We have alluded to the obvious difference between theology and the natural sciences. Nevertheless, they are in certain respects analogous and akin to each other, and we ought not to close this discussion without laying some emphasis upon this kinship. Great as the differences are, theology has in fact much in common with the spirit of the natural sciences. Indeed, I would venture to say that theology is closer to science than to what is sometimes called the philosophy of religion. The so-called philosophy of religion is simply a collective name for the various kinds of philosophy whose conclusions tend in a religious direction. At its best, it is another, and less specific name, for the kind of natural theology whose achievements we briefly assessed in the last chapter. But Christian theology is not itself a part of the philosophy of religion; it is a rational assessment and interpretation (with many prophetic, that is pragmatic, applications to the problems of human existence in the world) of those specifically Christian facts which constitute the special subject matter of theology. It is the possession of a special subject matter, a particular set of facts and experiences to the elucidation of which it devotes its energies, that distinguishes theology from philosophy of religion and that approximates it to the sciences. Theology, like the sciences, is grounded upon fact and experience, and, like the sciences, it must in the long run defer to them.

The underlying kinship between philosophy and the sciences is the true theme of Bishop Butler's great work *The Analogy of Religion.* This is a difficult book for the modern reader because it addresses itself to a particular eighteenth century controversy, that between what used to be called natural religion and revealed religion, a controversy which has long ceased to have any vitality or meaning. The eighteenth century is over, and its particular intellectual difficulties and scruples no longer trouble the conscience or the reason of contemporary man, whether Christian or not. The result is that Butler's book reads like a brilliant contribution to a dead controversy, meaningful no doubt in its own time but no longer meaningful to us or relevant to our needs and interests.

The book only comes alive if the reader translates it, so to speak, as he goes along, constantly asking himself what Butler would have said if he had written from the same point of view in our own time. His main point is that both science and theology are confronted at bottom with the same problems and the same difficulties, the problems with which the human mind is inevitably confronted when it ceases merely to elaborate its own ideas or to deduce the logical consequences of its own presuppositions, and instead disciplines itself to the scrutiny and interpretation of sheer fact. The difficulties, he tells us, which confront us when we seek to make sense of the data of revealed religion are fundamentally identical with the difficulties which confront us when we seek to think in naturalistic terms. There is an inevitable tension between reason and fact, whether the

146

facts which concern us are the natural facts with which the scientist deals, or the unique facts located in past time which are the subject matter of the historian, or the very special class of facts in and through which God has revealed himself to men (which are the special and proper objects of theological scrutiny). Reason, no doubt, would in one sense be happier if it were not compelled to saddle itself with the heavy discipline of deferring to the facts, if it felt itself free, as some philosophers have, to wander without constraint wherever the flow of ideas seemed to take it. On the other hand, reason inevitably craves a worthwhile subject matter, and such an absence of discipline as it sometimes seems to demand does in the end prove self-frustrating. It is by displaying its power to endure this endless tension between reason and fact that the human mind manifests its vitality and endurance. The recognition of the reality of this close parallel between the mood and method of theology and the mood and method of natural science should do much to help theologians and scientists understand and appreciate one another more adequately than they have tended to do in the recent past.

The Role of Theology in the History of Science

Another factor which may tell in the same reconciling direction is our new appreciation of the important place of theology in the story of the development of modern science as we now know it, particularly in its very early stages. Until recently, this particular aspect of the history of science was almost completely ignored, but contemporary research is making us more aware of it.

Most of the giants and heroes who dominate the story of the earlier phases of modern science were what we may call amateur theologians—Galileo and Boyle, for example, rather good ones, and Newton a very bad one. This suggests that in their minds there was no clear-cut break or cleavage between theological thinking and scientific thinking.

If we direct our search to an earlier period, to the later middle ages, we shall find people who concerned themselves sometimes with what would be called theological thinking and sometimes with what we should now call scientific themes. These did so without recognizing any fundamental difference between them at all. Thus, Robert Grosseteste, who taught at Oxford and subsequently became Bishop of Lincoln in the thirteenth century, is an important, without being a particularly great, figure in the story of the development of medieval theology and Christian philosophy. In the story of the early development of modern science, he is a supremely significant figure, in some ways more outstanding than the better-known Roger Bacon. His great achievement was the hammering out of a synthesis between the methods of pure rational analysis employed by the scholastic philosophers and the empirical trial and error methods employed by medieval inventors and technicians. (The rapid advance of technical development during the later middle ages is something which has also been overlooked in the more conventional history books.) This fusion of empirical and technical methods with techniques of pure rational analysis was perhaps the achievement which made the development of modern science, as we know it, possible; yet Grosseteste, himself, was apparently unaware of the way in which he was continually stepping out of the realm of what we should now call theology into the realm of what we should now call science. For him, these two worlds were one world, and their problems and perplexities all of one piece.

In the last resort, we may still hold that Grosseteste was right. There is in fact only one world, and theology and science are both concerned with the same world from different points of view. The distinction between them is obvious and important but not fundamental. It is certainly not a distinction which, once we understand it properly, need divide the theologian from the scientist either in sympathy or in spirit, nor should we permit it to blind us to their common history, their common roots in Christian civilization —characteristically and uniquely a spiritual civilization which treats the material, visible world with seriousness and reverence.

CHAPTER SIX

THE USEFULNESS AND GRANDEUR OF NATURAL THEOLOGY

There can be no fruitful communication between the Church and the world unless there is some coincidence of the range of interests of men in the Church with the range of interests of men in the world. Men can talk with one another only in a language which they all understand, and about things in which they share some common motivating interest.

I can think of no danger in the contemporary intellectual situation more alarming than the perceptible tendency of a certain kind of Christian intellectualism to become so inbred and introverted that it has nothing to say to the world about anything in which the world is interested, and no interest of its own that anybody outside Christianity can conceivably share. Here is a real danger that may turn Christian theology into no more than an interpretation of the private religious experience of the Christian man. Of course, different Christians will interpret the term, "private religious experience," in different ways. It may be interpreted from the evangelical point of view, existentially, as the experience of conversion and Christian existence in the sight of God; or it may be interpreted by the catholic primarily in terms of liturgical life and our participation in the corporate life of the Body of Christ; or, again, it may be interpreted primarily in terms of mysticism, as by the religious individualist. But however we interpret the meaning of the phrase, it is possible to concentrate upon it in so narrow and introverted a fashion as to make it appear irrelevant to the experience and range of interests of any man who is not a Christian.

A mere interpretation, however intelligent and profound, of experiences which we have and which the vast majority of other people do not have (so far as their conscious minds tell them) will not establish a platform for communication. The necessity of a common platform, of a Christian sharing in the interests of non-Christian men in the world, emphasizes the importance of natural theology. In order to communicate with the world, it is necessary to have something to communicate which can be understood in terms of the world's experience and intelligibly propounded in the world's language, and which is concerned with something about which those with whom we wish to communicate desire to hear.

That is why I cannot but feel that Dr. Paul Tillich's fondness for defining theology in terms of what he calls "ultimate concern" is a rather unhappy and unfortunate one. My quarrel is with the phrase itself rather than with what

Dr. Tillich appears to mean by it when he expounds his conception in detail. No doubt all men are ultimately concerned about something or other, and no doubt also the theologian is ultimately concerned about all that concerns him, which is, in a sense, everything. But as things are, we must admit that the question of ultimate concern is one which divides men and makes their ultimate concerns appear irrelevant to one another. What unites men and constitutes a sphere of discourse in which they can meet and communicate is what we may call the area of "proximate concern," the immediate problems which arise for all of us out of the common human condition in which we find ourselves. It is only by showing that Christianity and Christian theology are as much at home in the sphere of proximate concern as in the sphere of ultimate concern, have as much to say about the immediate problems of the human condition as about the ultimate reality of God and the ultimate destiny of man, that we can establish a point of communication with man as such.

Christian Intellectualism

Many well-meaning critics of Christian intellectualism are apt to charge the Christian theologians and intellectuals with using words which are too long and employing conceptions which are too subtle for the common man to understand. But that is not the real problem. Such a criticism is not really a criticism at all, for it says no more in effect than that Christian intellectuals are real intellectuals, which is just what they are meant to be and must be if they are to do their own special work in the Church effectively. It would be a lamentable thing, indeed, if the Christian intellectuals were no more than pseudo-intellectuals, concealing a fundamental intellectual naïveté beneath a thick covering of sophisticated language.

It is not, in the last analysis, long words and subtle conceptions which prevent communication between the mind of the Church and the mind of the world. Indeed, the use of everyday and imprecise language, and the employment of only a simple conceptual apparatus may well lead to a complete breakdown of communication in a world in which all the problems are exceedingly complicated. I remember a friend of mine telling me that he was once invited to preach in a London church whose congregation consisted very largely of members of Parliament, industrialists, bankers and people whose vocation in life compelled them to spend the week wrestling with vast, well-nigh unfathomable problems.

After the service a banker churchwarden remarked to my friend, in a mildly critical way, "You know, in some way I prefer a rather simple sermon about the simple Gospel."

My friend replied "What on earth would be the use of a simple gospel to a man like you?"

The churchwarden sighed and said rather wistfully, "I should find it very restful."

Of course, we can sympathize with the churchwarden, but the Christian Church cannot conceivably resign itself to proclaiming a restful gospel!

The real obstacle to communication is not long words or subtle conceptions. The problem lies elsewhere. What do we desire to communicate? Where do our interests converge and overlap with those of the people to whom we wish to speak? What have we got to say to men in the world about the things in which they are already interested? The real problem may be described as that of making a valid and fruitful transition from a merely devotional, Biblical, and churchly theology, which confines itself to working out and defining the basic theological concepts and categories, to a prophetic theology which openly employs them in the interpretation of the problems of human existence.

I do not wish to be misunderstood. Obviously, the task of discerning and defining the basic Biblical and theological concepts and categories is a very important theological discipline, indeed it is the primary function of the theologian. It is, in the last resort, his dedication to such an activity which constitutes him a theologian. But the basic theological concepts and categories are more than self-sufficient ideas which ask only to be exhibited in their purity and clarity before the respectful eyes of an admiring church. They are also hypotheses which require to be verified in terms of the experience of men in the world. Merely to discern and define the basic and primary Christian ideas and say in effect to the world, "Here they are, do not do anything with them—they may not be tough enough to bear the strain—confine yourself to inspecting them with a reverent gaze and from a decent distance," is hardly science, even in the rather special sense of the word in which theology may reasonably claim to be a science.

A real science fulfils itself and expresses its genius in the activity by means of which it verifies its hypotheses, its basic concepts, in terms of experience and experiment. The same

154

is true in theology. The verification of the validity of theological conceptions is to be found in a prophetic activity which manifests the power of theology to interpret and handle the world's problems, to unravel its perplexities and shed precious shafts of light on its dark places. Theology verifies itself in prophecy. This means that the theologian must be a man obsessed by an insatiable curiosity which prompts him to search into the nature of all that conditions human existence, to interest himself in everything in which he finds other men interested. Wherever and whenever the theologian addresses himself to his task in such a frame of mind, some kind of natural theology, some kind of theological concern for the natural, will inevitably manifest itself in his Christian thinking.

The Alternatives

What are the alternatives to this theological and prophetic approach to the problem of communication? As we look round on the very varied evangelistic activities which are being carried on in different parts of contemporary Christendom, we can indeed perceive several alternatives, most of them rather unpleasant and of doubtful validity.

There are, for example, the rather crude techniques—although here and there we find more sophisticated and refined versions of the same kind of thing—of those who are called revivalists. Their method is to hammer at people with a constantly reiterated, highly emotional presentation of the Gospel until the latter are battered into a kind of intellectual insensibility. Not unsimilar, are the activities of those, operating on more exalted social levels, who gather together their spiritual clientele at luxurious weekend house parties and morally challenge and gregariously herd them into a kind of self-conscious salvation.

The fundamental error of those who resort to methods of this kind is that they fail to display any proper reverence for intellectual integrity. They are disobedient to the Pauline injunction to think upon (that is, reverence) the things which are just, pure, true, lovely, and of good report. Intellectual integrity is not, of course, the only virtue, but it is undeniably a very noble one, and one which the modern world, at its best, has learned to respect very highly.

We must show ourselves capable of respecting, not only intellectual integrity wherever we find it, but also the modern world's respect for intellectual integrity. I believe it to be true that we can only speak profitably to men about their many sins if we show ourselves capable of appreciating their few virtues. We do not have to proclaim the Gospel in a world which is entirely black, devoid of one single redeeming feature. No doubt it would in some ways be easier to proclaim the Gospel if that were indeed the case, and we may wish, in a certain mood, that it were so. However, we must be realistic; it is not the case. A reverence for the very real virtue of intellectual integrity is one of the best characteristics of the contemporary mind. It is vitally important that we should share that reverence in our private minds and also make it outwardly visible that we do so. We do not desire that men should become Christian against their reasons, on the strength of an excess of religious emotion or by an arbitrary act of will. On the contrary, we desire that men should come to Christ with the whole of their being, and that means, among other things, with the free consent of their reason.

Again, there is a certain way of theologizing and proclaiming the Gospel which rather resembles the way in which a harping wife afflicts and sometimes dominates her husband. The preachers may appear to nag at the world, quarrelling with it as a matter of course, almost on principle, about whatever it does and whatever it is suffering. Some unwise parents treat their children in the same way. To the children themselves, it seems that they are the targets of an endless stream of criticism which falls upon them with equal weight whatever they do. The result is that real and important criticisms fail to make their point, because the children feel that their parents are against them anyway. There are some kinds of preaching and some kinds of theology which seem motivated by a kind of anger against the world. The theologian, especially, dare never forget that the wrath of the theologian is a very different thing from the wrath of God, and almost invariably unspiritual in its motivation.

We may recollect how the prophet Jonah was unwilling to go to Nineveh to preach the word of God there until he was told what his message was to be when he arrived: "Yet forty days and Nineveh shall be destroyed." This encouraging news overcame all his reluctance, because that was precisely the kind of thing he enjoyed saying in places like Nineveh. The mantle of Jonah seems to have fallen upon not a few contemporary theologians, but the prophet who prophesies in the spirit of Christ dare never pronounce a message of doom unless the pronunciation of it breaks his own heart. He dare never declare the judgment of the Lord upon mankind unless the judgment falls first and most heavily upon himself. The doom of the world is also the doom of the Church and the doom of the prophet. In any case, men do not and will not come to Christ merely in order to escape their doom. They come to Christ, if they come at all, in order to find and know the God made manifest in Christ. There is no other reason for becoming or being a Christian.

The Way of Natural Theology

Intellectual difficulties which prevent people from making the act of faith, in so far as they are honest and sincere, demand our sympathy and respect. The suggestion that men should be urged to overcome them by suppressing them, though it may seem to bear fruit in a surprisingly large number of cases, is always unwise, even in some ways immoral, and it is often self-frustrating in its ultimate consequences. An act of faith which is only made possible by the suppression of honest intellectual scruples results in a subsequent life of faith which will continually be weakened from within by the lurking presence of the suppressed intellectual doubts. Intellectual doubt cannot be suppressed; it can only be dissipated by careful intellectual analysis. In a way, natural theology may be likened to psychoanalysis. It seeks to disperse, by a process of patient and dispassionate analysis, the roots of doubt and those half-concealed, sometimes altogether unconscious, intellectual difficulties which prevent a man from coming to God, and offering himself to God, with a faith which comprehends his entire being.

158

Of course, an intellectual process of this kind will not of itself suffice to bring a man to God. It has frequently been noted that no man was ever argued into becoming a converted, committed Christian. That is true. It is equally true, however, that no honest man who has gone through a period of intellectual doubt—and few mentally alive people can grow up in our world without ever experiencing its sting—can become a Christian without any argument at all, although the argument may, in some cases, be a purely internal argument which takes place in his own mind.

Even though the argument which natural theology conducts never suffices by itself to turn men into convinced, converted Christians, it may nevertheless be necessary, in order to remove many of the impediments which must be removed before honest men feel able to become Christian with integrity. From this point of view, the argument of natural theology may be recognized as a process of great importance and significance. And to conduct that argument in the name of the Father and of the Son and of the Holy Ghost is indeed a very high office and vocation which no man should despise.

Natural Theology, an Unfinished Mission

If, then, it is essential to the nature of natural theology that it seizes with joy and avidity upon points of convergence, points at which for the moment it can feel itself at one with some current tendency, it follows that natural theology cannot be a fixed doctrine, written down once for all in a book in which it can be read and learned. What do people mean when they say, as some theologians do, "I do not believe in natural theology"? Does such a man mean, "I do not believe that it is natural to be theological, or I do not believe in being theological about nature"? He may of course mean these, but I think that he usually means, "I have seen certain propositions written in a book, purporting to be propositions in natural theology, with which I do not agree." So, of course, have we all. But, for that matter, we have all read in books propositions purporting to be propositions in revealed and Biblical theology with which we equally disagree.

Natural theology is not, and cannot be, a completed doctrine, something written down once and for all by a Thomas Aquinas or a Bishop Butler or some other distinguished worthy of the past. Natural theology, indeed, is a project rather than a doctrine, a process which in the nature of the case cannot be completed as long as time, and the debates of time, and our novelty-laden human experience shall continue. Natural theology is an essay in the art of communication, something which has to be renewed and rethought in every age, in the light of what the existing points of convergence happen to be at the time, and they certainly differ very greatly at different periods in the development of thought and civilization. Natural theology is always and necessarily contemporary theology. The different manifestations of its spirit hold for an age rather than for all time, though some of its greatest achievements may survive and bear restatement in new language again and again.

The natural theologian is a kind of missionary, and to become a natural theologian involves a kind of *kenosis,* the sort of self-emptying which we recognize supremely in the

160

Incarnation. ("Who being in the form of God emptied Himself.") The natural theologian, having at his disposal the whole treasury of revelation and theology and the Gospel, nevertheless seeks to empty his mind and stand for a time where other men stand, hoping to find his way back to his true home from where they are, and to bring some of them at least with him. This is no small operation of the spirit, and it finds its sanction in the very heart of the Gospel itself.

Thus some kind of natural theology, some kind of spiritual and intellectual mood and phase of the Church's life in which the Christian theologian empties himself, in order to discover his intellectual kinship with those who dwell outside the Christian community, is a necessary moment in the life and thought of the Church. So long as we find ourselves in a world which is always in theory, and sometimes in practice, intellectually honest, the Christian Church will never be able to dispense with its natural theology and its natural theologians. In any case, as I have also argued, no system of theology can ever be complete without its chapter entitled Natural Theology, for the God who stands self-revealed in the Gospel is the Creator of the world, and only when interpreted in the light of His loving purpose does the world and the life men live in the world disclose its real meaning and its eternal worth.

Graceful Reason

The word "graceful," understood in its true sense, means more than elegant and beautifully proportioned motion. To speak of graceful reason is not to ask the question whether reason is capable of a precision and economy of effort which makes the study of its operations an aesthetic delight. Incontestably it can, and I have often felt that to trace the masterly mental processes of a supreme artist in the use of reason, like Bishop Berkeley or St. Thomas Aquinas or Plato, is rather like listening to a great violinist performing almost magical wonders on his fiddle. But the title of this book speaks of "graceful reason" in a more profound and a more literal sense. Can reason indeed be filled with grace? Is it something in man which God can and does use? Is it in its own essential nature, and can it become in the living human use of it, an organ of spiritual experience, a means of sounding the depths of our intercourse with God, and then of deepening them still further?

When we understand what the New Testament means by grace, we see at once that, although all human things are made for grace, no human thing can attain grace in its own right. The grace of God is something which has continually to be poured by God into the human vessel, something which men can only possess if God gives it to them. We can only be graceful if we are filled with grace. Is reason just such a receptacle?

This book is nothing if it is not an attempt to show that we may give an affirmative answer to precisely this question. Reason is more, and not less, rational when it takes for its proper theme the truth of God, when it seeks to unite the truth which we find in the gospel in one synthesis with the many truths with which life in the world is continually confronting us. There is no truth but truth, and the many truths will not finally coalesce into one truth until the last day, until that consummation in which the meaning of everything will be laid bare. Meanwhile, loyalty to the truth displays itself in the searching rather than in the finding, and the life of reason is one in which we observe with joy and admiration the truths we know coalescing into unities before our very eyes. And such provisional unities as we do observe point always toward that ultimate unity which is presented to us in the Christian revelation and which, in satisfying the entire being of the Christian man, satisfies his reason also.

Well may we cry, as we contemplate the insight and fruitfulness of even inadequate and sin-stained reason in a fallen world, and particularly where we see it rising to its height in consecrated service to the truth of God:

Hail Reason, Full of Grace!

102-354-c-5